Spirit-Controlled
FAMILY LIVING

Spirit-Controlled
FAMILY LIVING

Tim and Bev LaHaye

Fleming H. Revell Company
Old Tappan, New Jersey

Library of Congress Cataloging in Publication Data

LaHaye, Tim F
    Spirit-controlled family living.

    Bibliography: p.
    1. Family—Religious life. I. LaHaye,
Beverly, joint author. II. Title.
BV4526.2.L28   249   78-13526
ISBN 0-8007-0950-0
ISBN 0-8007-0951-9 pbk.

Contents

Introduction

Bev and I have not always been happily married. For several years our relationship so deteriorated that we didn't communicate very often, and even then we irritated each other. On a scale of 0–100, I would have rated our marriage about 25; Bev says it was more like 30. The only things that held us together were (1) rejection of divorce as a solution; (2) four children; (3) vocational necessity (divorce would have ruined my career—churches take a dim view of employing divorced ministers); (4) Phlegmatic stubbornness and Choleric determination. Bev was too stubborn to admit defeat, and I was too bullheaded to give up. Does that sound happy? It certainly wasn't!

Strangely enough, we were both very dedicated Christians. Telling it now, I realize it doesn't sound like it, but we really were. We met in a fine Christian college where we were preparing to serve the Lord. Bev dedicated her life to Christ when she was fourteen, hoping someday to serve as a missionary. At a summer camp, when I was fifteen, I had surrendered to the call to preach the Gospel. Bev finished high school early, so she was only seventeen when I met her at the dinner table the fourth week into our freshman year. I had done a two-year stretch in the Air Force and was twenty at the time.

We didn't fall in love at first sight, but I was a rather

determined young man; so even though she was afraid to show too much interest in me at first, we gradually fell in love. I kept after her and finally convinced her that "it was the Lord's will" that we get married the following July, long before either of us was mature enough. But who can tell two young people in love to "slow down"? My mother couldn't, and neither could Bev's parents.

During our junior year in school we were called to a little country church in the South Carolina mountains, where we served the Lord for two years, and my parishioners graciously displayed the spirit of long-suffering as they allowed me to practice my first batch of sermons. After graduation I prayed desperately that our two-year growth from an average attendance of seventy-five to one of seventy-seven was not a true picture of my preaching ability.

As newlyweds enjoying the challenge of our first church, life was exciting and dynamic. Except for financial difficulties, we didn't have many problems those first three years. Linda, our firstborn, came during that time, and we both loved her dearly. Except for a few of Bev's periods of stubborn silence which followed my occasional eruptions of anger, we got along fairly well. I'd score our marriage about 85 percent for the first few years.

Somehow, in the providence of God, we were miraculously called to pastor the Minnetonka Community Church in a suburb of Minneapolis. A delightful six years ensued (except for the 200,000 tons of snow I was forced to shovel). The church, which was constituted of some of the finest people in the world, grew from 90 in Sunday school to almost 400. I was busy with two lengthy building programs in my first full-time pastorate, and Bev was active as a pastor's wife, Junior Department superintendent, and young mother of three (our two boys were born there). I would score those years about 90 percent for our ministry and 70 percent for our marriage.

Our call to the Scott Memorial Baptist Church of San Diego, California—twenty-two years ago—was another act of God's providence. Two years later, Lori was born—but even then our marriage relationship was going downhill. We kept up a good front and always did the "right thing," but although we experienced many happy times, they were occurring at increasingly detached intervals and were accompanied by a heightened amount of tension. By the time we were ten to twelve years into marriage, we had become two strong-willed personalities of the opposite sex who lived in the same house, shared the same children, and held the same basic spiritual views and values—but disagreed on almost everything else. As Bev matured, she refused to be bullied into doing what she didn't want to, and the more she balked, the more dominating I became. We won't bore you with the gory details—they were similar to those of millions of other unhappy couples.

The strangest part of all is that we were both very dedicated Christians and tireless servants of a very fine Bible-believing church. In fact, the church was growing well, and people were receiving Christ regularly, forcing us to plunge into two building programs in four years and eventually to expand to three Sunday-morning services. The folks seemed to enjoy my expository preaching with its strong emphasis on practical Christian living.

But something was missing! We knew absolutely nothing about the Spirit-controlled life, particularly at home. We could live the Christian life away from home, because difficult circumstances came in shorter and less-pressured doses. But at home the pressures became too intense, and when we failed to control ourselves, we compounded the problem. Many folks have the mistaken idea that pressure *makes* one's spirit. That isn't true; it only *reveals* your spirit. Actually, what you are under pressure is what you are! We were deteriorating under family pressure, and so was our marriage.

At a time when our marriage score was hovering between a percentage rating of 25 and 30, Bev received an invitation to attend a Gospel Light Sunday School Conference at the beautiful Forest Home conference grounds. That week she had the life-changing experience of being filled or controlled with the Holy Spirit. She called me on Wednesday and enthusiastically urged me to come up for the last day. Since she had been away from home four days, our marriage relationship had jumped to about 35 percent, so I reluctantly accepted. What I didn't realize was that the speakers had addressed her biggest problem the first of the week, but had switched to mine the last two days. I arrived just in time to hear Dr. Henry Brandt tell the story of my life. Oh, he was referring to another angry Choleric minister who had come to him from the Mayo Clinic with bleeding ulcers (I only had pains in my stomach which I refused to take to the doctor), but I recognized its applicability. When Brandt finished, I admitted what an angry, selfish hypocrite I had been, so I slipped out of the chapel, got alone with God, and for the first time in my adult life was filled with the Holy Spirit. I didn't see any visions and I made no audible sounds, but I underwent a life-changing experience with God. Because Bev and I came down from that mountain filled with the Holy Spirit, He changed our marriage, family, and ministry. Gradually our selfishness, my anger, Bev's fears, and our joint bullheadedness have been replaced by the love, joy, and peace which the Holy Spirit provides when we are controlled by Him.

Today we can honestly say that we enjoy the most ideal marriage relationship two people can share on this earth. When in 1968 I wrote *How to Be Happy Though Married,* which God has been pleased to use in helping over 600,000 people (assuming one reader per copy), I dedicated the book to Bev with these words:

> This book is lovingly dedicated to my wife, Beverly. Her patient understanding and loving tenderness have made our marriage an increasingly joyous experience. Her inner beauty, "the hidden woman of the heart," like her physical beauty, has improved through these twenty years. Every day I thank God for bringing her into my life.

That statement is even more true today than when first written. Now I would add, "She has become my dearest friend."

We are convinced that the Holy Spirit's filling is the key to happy family living, for that is the context of Ephesians 5. It is certainly the way He worked in our own marriage. However, we have observed that most Christians go to one of two extremes regarding the filling of the Holy Spirit, thus missing the practical purpose for which He has come into their lives. They either concentrate on an emotionally oriented experience that centers on themselves, or they ignore Him altogether. As we shall show in this book, the Bible teaches that the Holy Spirit's filling is really for family living, not for what they do at church. In fact, we tell people to examine their conduct at home to see if they are really filled with the Holy Spirit. For if we can live the Spirit-controlled life at home, we can live it anywhere. Why? Because what we are at home is what we really are!

If your conduct at home during the past two weeks offered little evidence that you were filled or controlled (they mean the same) with the Holy Spirit, then you aren't filled with Him—regardless of what the people at church or work think of you. Ask yourself this question: "If the members of

my family were secretly polled on whether or not I was
filled with the Spirit during the past two weeks, what would
they say?'' That is the best indication of whether or not you
are.

God the Holy Spirit always enriches and beautifies the
life He fills. What better gift can He bestow upon a Christian than to make his home the most wonderful place on
earth? And that is exactly what He wants to do for all His
children. We have lived both ways and thus can testify that
Spirit-controlled family living is the only way to live. No
doubt that is the reason God has given us a ministry of
sharing the Spirit-controlled life for family living with thousands of people around the world. He says in His Word that
we are able to comfort others with the same comfort we
ourselves are comforted by God (2 Corinthians 1:4).

Seven years ago God specifically led us to found Family
Life Seminars, never dreaming where such a decision
would lead. At first I conducted Friday evening and all-day
Saturday seminars on family living wherever five pastors in
a city invited me. Bev stayed with the children at home,
where she would conduct a woman's retreat while I acted as
father. Then for three years I teamed up with Dr. Henry
Brandt and later with Dr. Howard Hendricks. In all we
conducted a hundred and fifty seminars in sixty-eight cities
of the United States and Canada. Two years ago our
youngest child went off to a Christian college, and Bev was
free to travel with me and share in the seminars. Since then
we have conducted an additional sixty-five seminars in
forty-two countries of the world, relating principles of the
Spirit-controlled life for families to well over a hundred
thousand people. The mail we have received from many
who attended has confirmed that lives have been transformed after being filled with the Holy Spirit and using His
power to apply the biblical principles for marriage and the
family.

During the past year, the press of other duties forced us to limit our seminars to population centers where at least twenty-five ministers have invited us, and we have enjoyed an average attendance of over fifteen hundred. At first we weren't sure how the pastors and churches would receive a woman lecturer, but in the providence of God, Bev's ministry has actually drawn a greater response than we expected. Apparently, in this "day of the woman," it has helped to see a husband-and-wife team share in such a program. Now we are in the process of launching a new film ministry of four one-hour lectures taken at our San Diego seminar. These have been prepared for local churches to use in the training of their families and as a tool to bring in the un-saved of their community who are interested in building a strong homelife. Only God knows where this ministry will lead, but we are convinced of two things today: (1) people (within and without the church) are vitally interested in the family; (2) the Bible contains the principles they need to enjoy a happy family life.

This book—not a repetition of our other writings—contains those principles that we teach at our seminars. It particularly emphasizes the ministry of the Holy Spirit in the homelife of the Christian. Some of the chapters will be written by Bev, some by me, and others we will share. Forgive us if we relate personal stories to illustrate biblical principles, but we want you to know that God's plan really works. It has for us, and it will for you. This is really the first book we have written this way, and we trust it will illustrate what God the Holy Spirit has done with our lives, blending us together so that we can accomplish more work as partners than either of us could separately. It is our prayer that He will do the same for you.

1

The Importance
of the Family

The family is the most important single factor in the molding of a human being. It either prepares him to reach for his ultimate destiny and fulfillment, or it cripples and inhibits him from attaining his original potential. When a society disregards its families, it suffers irreparable loss. If it disregards its families long enough, it passes into oblivion like many ancient civilizations of the past.

The first institution God founded was the family. In fact, He established only three institutions—the home or family, government, and the church. These three institutions form the basic building blocks of a sane and well-ordered society.

Family. The family (Genesis 2:18–25) was to provide a haven for its members to prepare to enter society and serve God and their fellowman.

Government. Human government was founded by God (Genesis 9:4–7; 10:5; Romans 13:1–8) for the purpose of protecting man from those depraved individuals who either had not learned in their family—or refused to obey—God's principles of respect for others and their property, so necessary to civilization.

15

Church. The church was instituted many centuries later because the family and government had both failed so miserably to protect man from himself and his fellowman. The basic sin of self-will and selfishness in the human heart had brought society to a place where most human beings were slaves of other human beings. Into such a sinful environment God sent His Son Jesus Christ to die for man's sin, that he might be "born again," gaining a new nature which would enable him to follow the time-honored principles for achieving the happiness and fulfillment in life which God had revealed in His Word. To communicate these principles He founded His church. The primary purpose of the church which Jesus Christ promised to build was the teaching of the Gospel and the commandments of God (Matthew 28:18–20).

Whenever the church has done her work positively, she has so strengthened her families that they have served as a stabilizing influence in society, producing freedom, liberty, and opportunity unequaled in any of the pagan cultures of the world. When the church has failed in her teaching role, it has been at the expense of both the family and society.

Today the best marriages and families are found in Christian homes whose members actively attend churches which teach biblical principles for family living. The young people from such homes are the leadership hope for tomorrow. As president of a Christian college, I am thrilled to see the sterling young people who come to us from many Christian homes. I am aware of today's general family breakdown that is even making serious inroads into the church, but I am also aware that many Christian homes are stronger and better than they have ever been.

The home and the church are not competitive but naturally supportive institutions. In fact, if it had not been for the church, humanists of our day—with their teachings of "no absolutes" and "do what you feel like doing"—would have destroyed our culture. Placing little or no value on the home, if they had their way, they would abolish it and allow government to raise the children. That may be appropriate for mind control, but it is certainly destructive of freedom, happiness, and fulfillment. Anything that is harmful to the home is the enemy of society, and humanism has become our culture's most destructive family force today.

The Family Is Basic to Adults

The family was God's first institution because it is basic. Man by himself is incomplete. Almost everyone is familiar with the story in Genesis 2 of lonely Adam and his naming of the animals who came before him. The passage concludes with the words: ". . . but for Adam there was not found an help meet for him." Then we read the beautiful story of God's special provision, for He took from Adam a rib, made the woman, and "brought her unto the man" (Genesis 2:20–22). Many theological romanticists suggest that this was the world's first wedding and that God performed the first marriage ceremony. From that day to this, no other factor in human life has been more significant than the home.

In my book *How to Win Over Depression*, I cited the twenty-five-year study of stress on human beings by Dr. Thomas Holmes of the University of Oregon. He listed forty-three crises that occur in life, according to their severity in producing stress. Not until two years after the book was published did I notice something extremely significant about his list. The top 50 percent of life's stress-producing problems related directly to the home. Consider the first ten items listed below:

Rank	Crisis	Points
1	Death of a spouse	100
2	Divorce	73
3	Marital separation	65
4	Jail term	63
5	Death of close family member	63
6	Personal injury or illness	53
7	Marriage	50
8	Job firing	47
9	Marital reconciliation	45
10	Retirement	45

Except for a physical injury (to which he ascribed fifty-three points) six of the top seven traumas of life have to do with family disruption (assuming that a jail term separates family members). According to Dr. Holmes, family problems are at least twice as stress producing as others—and in many cases three or four times as great. Of his forty-three common problems in life, I counted twenty-three that related to the family.

One conclusion we can draw from this crisis chart is that family problems cause us the most stress because the family is the most important factor in our lives. Show me a person who enjoys dynamic family life, and I will show you a basically happy person. In fact, family fulfillment leads to life fulfillment. But without family fulfillment nothing else in life really matters.

What could possibly cause successful businessmen, or great geniuses who receive world renown, to spend their final years in despair? Usually it is because they became alienated from their families. And more often than not, they sacrificed family to gain notoriety. That is a price too great for any adult to pay, particularly in terms of a lifetime investment.

The Family Is Basic to Children

A child's family is easily the most important single influence in his life. Nothing else even runs a close second. The home molds character and personality. Inherited temperament makes a significant contribution, to be sure, but the direction which temperament takes is dependent on a person's homelife and training. For example, if two Choleric infants are born into contrasting families, they will grow up to be entirely different. Both will be active, hard-driving individuals, but the one from a rejecting home, where he watches his father rebel against authority, will more than likely turn out to be a gangster who takes advantage of his fellowman. The lad who grows up in a loving home, where values are communicated and laws are respected, is likely to become a very productive adult who makes a significant contribution to society.

The family histories of Max Jukes and Jonathan Edwards provide a startling illustration of this contrast. Max Jukes, who lived in the state of New York, did not believe in Christian training and married a girl of like character. From this union 1,026 descendants have been studied. Three hundred of them died prematurely. One hundred were sent to the penitentiary for an average of thirteen years each. One hundred and ninety became public prostitutes, and there were one hundred drunkards. On today's economic scale, the family cost the state over six million dollars. There is no record that they made any positive contribution to society.

Jonathan Edwards, who resided in the same state, believed in Christian training and married a woman of like mind. From this union 729 descendants have been studied. Three hundred became preachers of the Gospel. There were sixty-five college professors, thirteen university presidents, sixty authors of good books, three United States congressmen, and one vice-president of the United States. It is impossible to underestimate the contributions this family made to the state of New York and to the country. The Edwards family is a sterling example of the biblical principle: "Train up a child in the way he should go: and when he is old, he will not depart from it" (Proverbs 22:6). In spite of the enormous influence that TV and education exercise over the moral values and character of our children, nothing is more influential than the home and family . . . .

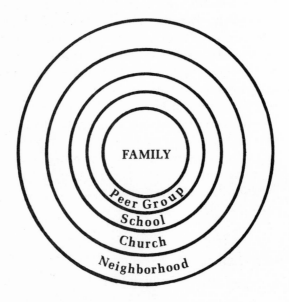

The diagram above indicates that although other important factors shape a child at various stages of life, none of them is more influential than the home. Thus, it is rightfully located in the center of the circle, for the home serves as the core of character building. This should be reassuring to Christian parents, who wonder if they can raise their children properly in this day of degeneracy and evil. One young couple protested, "We aren't going to have children; things are so socially corrupt that we refuse to bring a child into the world for fear of losing him to the world." We quickly countered that their position reflected complete unbelief in the power of God to use their Christian home to prepare the child for life. Let's face it—life offered little sweetness and light in the first century either, but Christians married and raised fine families and they took over the western world in less than three hundred years. Many excellent young people are being produced by active Christian families today. Of course, we possess assets unknown by the first-century Christian, such as a vital church influence on both parents and young people.

THE INFLUENCE OF EARLY CHILDHOOD

Moral values and character

Security and self-confidence—
Early months

A sense of curiosity—Early months
(some say <u>hours</u>)

Self-control—By 3-4 years of age

Sexual direction—By 3-5 years of age

Future sexual capability—By 6-8
years of age

The preceding diagram lists some of the profound influences on a child which affect his entire life. Moral values and character are not taught; they are "caught" in the home. A child whose parents demonstrate respect for the rights of others grows up with a healthy attitude toward his fellowman. If he sees his parents lie and cheat, he will do likewise.

The child who is loved intimately from day one will be far more secure (within the framework of his temperament) than if rejected. A study of children taken from their mothers at birth in the hospital and not returned until six hours later for their first feeding showed them far less curious and alert at one month than those placed in the arms of the mother as soon as both were cleaned up. Some doctors have determined that long periods of sterilized separation are emotionally harmful to the newborn. Obviously, God intended the newborn to go right from the mother's warm womb to her warm body. In such areas, modern medicine is seldom an improvement on nature, for researchers have discovered that breast-fed baby boys are far less likely to stutter at five or six years of age than those raised on a bottle. Even the doctors who made the study were not sure whether the distinction was the result of the more powerful mouth muscles developed through breast-feeding, or stronger and better emotional confidence due to love, closeness, and "stroking."

In the counseling room, I have repeatedly encountered the effect of a bad homelife upon sexual dysfunction. When I counsel a frigid wife, I look first for a rejecting father in her childhood. Show me a little girl of five or six who can run into her daddy's heart, sit on his lap, and kiss him any time she likes, and in fifteen or twenty years I will show you a young woman who is emotionally prepared to be a sexually responsive wife. Show me a little girl whose father rejects her spontaneous expressions of affection, and I will show you a girl with a predisposition toward frigidity before she is six to eight years of age.

The best sex education occurs long before a child's first day of school. Two parents who love each other in the home and demonstrate this affection almost never raise frigid or homosexual children. During the research for *The Unhappy Gays,* my book on homosexuality, I discovered why so many people have bought the lie that they are "born that way." Because the signs appear so early in life, they *think* it was a result of birth. Actually, their sex direction was usually predisposed before they were three years of age by a rejecting father and a domineering or smothering mother. The best preventive against homosexuality in either a boy or girl is a wholesome love relationship with the parent of the opposite sex and a positive role model by the parent of the same sex. Masculine fathers who love and spend time with their sons never saw them become homosexuals until recently. (Today there is so much propaganda and encouragement given the practice that many young people experiment with it until it becomes a learned behavior. Under these circumstances almost anyone can be swept into it. But even then the best preventive is a good homelife.)

It has long been observed that angry, hostile parents produce angry, hostile young people. Polite, gracious parents similarly reproduce themselves in the lives of their children. Doubtless that is the reason the teenager who stands out in my mind as the most thoughtful, considerate, and polite youngster I've ever known came from a home where her mother was equally gracious. "A chip off the old block" is more than an expression. It is a truism. And provided the "block" is what it should be, the "chip" will be right.

Marriage Is Basic to the Family

Although a close parent-child relationship is extremely important, it is not the principal basis for a good home. God instituted the family—marriage first and then children. Somehow today the emphasis has shifted until we have established child-centered homes. This is a mistake. Good marriages are primary to good homes. If you mistakenly sacrifice the marriage for the children, in so doing you will destroy both. Children understand by nature that they are number two in the hearts of their parents. And if we analyze their status within the home, we discover that it is transitory at best. Youngsters are destined to spend only five years in intimate dependence on the parents and then for the next fifteen years gradually grow independent of them. By contrast, parents are destined to spend upwards of fifty years together and will be joined to each other (under ordinary circumstances) the rest of their lives. A child then, almost from his inception, is being readied for graduation. In a home where he is given a number-two love priority, any child will flourish.

The worst emotional basket cases I have dealt with among young people were not rejected by their parents, but had become substitute lovers or, because of an inadequate marital love, had been subjected by a love-starved parent to a "smother" mother/father (or number one) love. A tragic illustration came to our attention recently. After eight years of marriage and two children, a wife began complaining about those long evening telephone calls when her husband would lie across the bed and recount to his mother every detail of the day. Eventually, she went into his room to find that he had moved out, leaving only this note: "I don't want to be married any longer. I am returning to live with my mother. She is still the number-one woman in my life."

Smother mother love had done it again—generated by a selfish compulsion to keep her son for herself.

In the last four years, Bev and I have traveled in five Communist countries of Eastern Europe and noted a basic similarity. The stronger the Communist party, the less freedom and more drab and disillusioning the life-style. But the people had one thing in common. Whether they went five months without meat, as they did in Russia, or whether they had to line up hours in advance on a cold day just to buy a pair of crudely manufactured shoes, there was one special object which even the Communists couldn't take from them—their family. Whether in a drab twenty-by-twenty unheated apartment or just a single room, they shared their lives with each other. The Communists know that the most volatile ingredient in causing a revolution in their country would be the senseless breakup of home and family.

This year we saw a beautiful illustration of the importance of the home. The delightful old lady who waited on our table in a Romanian hotel's restaurant had become quite friendly with us in spite of our language barrier. Usually quite somber in her sad and backward surroundings, we saw her eyes light up as a young woman in her early twenties walked up and kissed her warmly. The young lady, turning to us with a most pleasant smile on her face and an arm around the portly woman, proudly announced, "Me mama." That look spoke volumes! As long as you have someone who loves you, someone who cares whether you live or die, life is worth living—even under Communism.

Next to God Himself, nothing is more important in your life than your family. Are you giving it that kind of priority?

2
The Decline
of the Family

"Our civilization is headed for collapse if we don't start caring more for children and strengthening our family life," warned two nationally known experts on human development. Dr. Harold Voth of the famed Menninger Foundation elaborated, "I honestly believe that civilization as we know it is imperiled by the forces that are eroding the family. The American family is deteriorating because of the social and economic stress, and today's child is growing up alienated, frustrated and bored." But that isn't all they concluded. One predicted a chain reaction that could have devastating results on our culture: "Unless this trend is halted, children growing up today will have trouble forming families of their own—and the problem will perpetuate itself." He went on to say that of all the problems facing Americans today—energy, unemployment, pollution, Communism—none are more pressing than the crises in our family life. "Destroy the internal structure of the family and you are going to wreck civilization."

This pessimistic appraisal is not unrelated to the latest divorce statistics. In 1976 we crossed the one-million-divorce mark for the first time. In 1977 we crossed it again and added almost thirty thousand more. We can expect to exceed the million figure by another hundred thousand in 1978—or come very close. Experts warn that for every official divorce there is at least one "poor man's divorce," that is, when a man will not or cannot afford an attorney, he just runs away from his family and his responsibilities.

Sociologists estimate that currently ten to eleven million children are being raised by one parent due to divorce. It is further predicted that twenty-five to thirty million will be raised by a single divorced parent for at least part of their first eighteen years of life. One best-selling author suggests that the pressures of life have become so intense today— because of the rapidity of change—that it is wrong to think about remaining married for fifty years. He proposes that the average person divorce and remarry every ten years. That certainly would provide "change," but would it result in improvement?

Of the forty-four countries we have traveled in, no other nation comes even close to approximating the wonderful life-style we enjoy. It is hard to believe that its most important institution, the family, is on the brink of extinction. In my lifetime the divorce rate has risen from 27 percent to the latest high of 44.2 percent. (Among the under-twenty-one age group it is over 50 percent!) Marital instability has become so prevalent that a group of psychiatrists at a meeting in Los Angeles concluded that—since there is no solution to the constantly increasing divorce rate—they could only suggest that we "abolish marriage."

These social planners (or wreckers, depending on your point of view) forget one important fact. Man didn't think up marriage on his own. Unattached men and women didn't live for centuries in communal groups, then meet in a cave somewhere and decide to initiate the new and exciting concept of marriage. No, it was instituted by God when only one man and one woman were present on the earth. Therefore, it is basic to society.

Signs of Moral Collapse

It is interesting to compare conditions in our country currently with those of Greece and Rome just before their decline. They are tragically similar . . . .

1. Departure from their original religious beliefs
2. Obsession with a desire for recreation
3. Inflationary spiral which made the purchase of a home prohibitive for the average couple just starting out
4. Widespread sexual infidelity and a sharp rise in homosexuality
5. A constant clamor for democracy
6. Decline in child births so that the population did not replace itself. (The latest report indicates we now have 1.6 children per family, down from 2.4 just ten years ago.)

Have you ever wondered why this once-great nation, built largely on the principles of the Bible, began to imitate the pagan nations that finally destroyed themselves? It didn't originate with a single choice but with a series of decisions.

Eight Causes for Today's Family Breakdown

1. Dominance of atheistic, anti-Christian humanism in schools and media. At one time America boasted the world's greatest system of education, thanks largely to Christians. Harvard, Princeton, and Yale, colleges originally founded to train ministers to preach the Gospel, were the headwaters of education, providing the nation with qualified educators steeped in biblical concepts for living. About two hundred years ago, the Unitarians with their spirit of higher criticism took over Harvard, which eventually became the primary teaching source for teachers. Toward the end of the nineteenth century, our bright young educators were sent to Europe to get Ph.D. degrees, and they brought back European rationalism, socialism, and existentialism. In the early twenties, John Dewey and his cohorts succeeded in making Columbia University the nation's primary source for educators. As a citadel for atheistic humanism, "anti" everything that is Christian, Columbia gradually took over, ideologically, the nation's school system—until today the Bible, on which it was once founded, is the only thing you cannot study in the public school. Our young are taught everything from evolution to witchcraft at taxpayers' expense, but anything moral, wholesome, or supportive of righteous values is ridiculed. Since many educators believe man is "an animal," they seem obsessed with making him try to live like one. Consequently, free love, drugs on demand, rebellion against society, and anything harmful to the human mind is often advocated or at least presented as "acceptable" behavior. Currently the public school is bankrupt morally, socially, and educationally.

Whenever I review the present status of American education, uninformed parents and naive educators become defensive and take issue with me. But knowledgeable Christians in the secular system verify that I am not exaggerating. In fact, many have said, "You're not telling the half of it." Recently our Christian High School, the largest of its kind in California and perhaps the largest in the nation, took a survey of the professions of the parents who send their children to our school. Would you believe that the number-one answer was "secular education"? Because they know how corrupt it is, they send their children to our Christian school.

The liberal anti-Christian universities produce the journalists, playwrights, communications grads, and so on who work in the media—TV, radio, newspaper, and magazines. Is it any wonder that the media bombards our homes with the same perverted philosophy that subverts our youth in schools? Society with a live-like-an-animal mentality will soon destroy itself, and we are rapidly becoming that kind of society. An alarming illustration that the media are more interested in destroying the minds of our people than making money recently came to light. Last fall, a TV network launched a degenerate program exalting lesbianism, wife swapping, free love, homosexuality, and every other form of perversion. Ninety percent of the sponsors dropped the show, but rather than admit that they had produced a box-office flop, the network castigated the sponsors and went out looking for replacements. Although the top ratings go to clean family shows, network executives seem primarily interested in destroying the last vestige of morality and decency in this nation. Those without a strong moral fiber grounded in basic Christian teachings are often deceived by secular entertainment standards, much to their own and the nation's detriment.

2. Immorality and promiscuity. Nothing is more devastating to marriage and the home than infidelity. The obsession with sex in advertising, education, movies, and other media exalts infidelity until it has increased at an alarming rate.

3. Legalization of pornography. Ever since the Supreme Court, in effect, legalized pornography in the name of "freedom of speech and freedom of the press," it has come out from under the counter in a brown wrapper until now it is big business for *Playboy, Playgirl* and other emotionally inflammatory publications. Such material only activates the

mind to "think evil continually." The crime rate, including
forcible rapes and homosexual acts, rises in direct proportion to the increase in mind-corrupting pornography.

4. Women in the work force.   Since World War I, women in
the work force have increased from 2 percent to perhaps 49
percent of today's married women. This puts an abnormal
temptation before both sexes. It is quite common for married couples to spend more working hours a week in a close
relationship with someone else's spouse than with their
own. Many, of course, cannot resist this temptation. One of
the current fads is the renting of motel rooms for a two-hour
lunch break.

5. Easy divorce.   The modern "throw-away marriage," as
Alvin Toffler puts it, makes divorce easy. Ever since the
courts recognized the "no-fault divorce" with only a six-
month waiting period, marital breakups have increased
alarmingly. A judge who spent most of his judicial life presiding over divorces warned that "most people rush too
quickly into the divorce court. In my opinion fully one-third
of all the divorces I have granted could have been avoided if
the couple had sought the counsel of a third party instead of
my courtroom."

6. The permissive philosophy of the last generation.   The
nonbiblical child-raising concepts of Dr. Benjamin Spock
and his followers—who announced that permissivism encouraged creativity, and thus a child should be given the
right to express himself—have proven a dismal failure.
They have produced a whole generation of selfish, incon-
siderate, undisciplined adults too immature ever to
marry—but who do so anyway. They reject, abuse, or
abandon their children, and when the going gets tough they
bail out. Roughly 42 percent of such fathers are behind in

their support payments or quit paying altogether within two years, and another 20 percent join them three years later. Dr. Spock admitted his mistake back in 1974, advocating that parents return to disciplining their children, but that was too late for many of today's undisciplined parents. Most likely they will raise a crop of adults more emotionally scarred and love starved than themselves. They can only be helped by a genuine conversion to Christ, followed by a desire to establish their home environment and child treatment on biblical principles.

7. Urbanized man. All over the world people are migrating toward the city. Somehow man believes that his fortune will be found in the next big city, so he leaves his homeland or base, relatives, and friends and takes up a whole new way of life. This produces families with minimal roots and an absence of established social morals. In addition, it propels them into a foreign environment with none of their basic principles to guide them. Life in the big city may be more exciting for a time, but it certainly is not necessarily better. Man often loses contact with both nature and the type of mankind with whom he was born.

8. The Women's Lib morality. In the name of equal rights for women, a whole new life-style is creeping into America's family domain, one that is weakening the father's role in the home at the expense of the marriage and the family. Feminine-dominated homes are on the increase at an alarming rate, compounding the tragedies of marriage and the home. The irony of it is that American women already have better rights than do women in any country of the world. The ERA (Equal Rights Amendment) could be both a farce and a tragedy if it passes the required number of state legislatures. In the name of equal-employment opportunities, it might open the door to a rise in unemployment, discontinuance of alimony and child support, and even forced homosexual employment. It may even cause many mothers to lose the custody of their young to the father. Another irony is that the ERA will probably not provide one woman a single employment opportunity or right that is not already guaranteed by the portions of the Civil Rights Act already passed by the U.S. Congress. But it *will* contribute to the breakdown of the home.

Careerism for women has already brought many to the point of conflict between commitment to a career and a commitment to motherhood. Science has made it possible for women to prevent conception or delay having children so long that it becomes physically dangerous to have them at all. As Toffler said, "We are about to kill off the mystique of motherhood." This generation will someday marshall an army of unfulfilled women in their fifties and sixties. By the thousands they are cheating themselves and their husbands out of the most important blessing in life, a family.

Other reasons for the breakdown of the home include mobility, technology, and sin. So pessimistic have many critics of American life become that one expert on the family has stated grimly, "The family is near the point of complete extinction." Another popular writer adds, "Except for child raising the family is dead." But these prognosticators are wrong. The collapse of our society due to the dying condition of its families is already alerting and motivating people to do something about it. In spite of the above gloomy picture, there is hope.

The Remedy to Family Breakdown

Those who predict the demise of the family have not reckoned with the power of God. The spiritual renewal going on in the churches of our land is producing a whole new life-style, including a wholesome emphasis upon the family. Some of the best family-life instruction that has ever been written is coming from churches and Christian publishers. A recent visit to our local Christian bookstore revealed that books on the family comprise the largest category of new materials and best-sellers. Many concerned individuals outside the church recognize that Christians enjoy the most stable homes in the community and are looking to us for help. The new and growing interest in the family provides today's alert church with the best evangelistic opportunity in decades. The following suggestions provide very practical steps that will go a long way toward stopping the decline of the family.

1. Win the lost to Christ.   Every evangelistic church can furnish illustrations of an individual who has received Christ and, upon returning to his or her home, watched God gradually transform it. Just last Sunday evening a young father of four shared with our congregation how Christ had changed and revitalized his family since his conversion eighteen months ago. Then he proceeded to tell of a business associate he had led to Christ just two days before. Evangelism is the best way I know to refashion the homes of America. Only Jesus Christ can heal the wounds, bind the hurts, and give the wisdom necessary to raise the kind of children who will produce strong families for the next generation.

2. Establish a new Christian school system.   The present school system is so controlled by the federal government and misled or even corrupt educators that there is little hope of salvaging it. In my opinion, the only remedy is for churches and Christians to build a new church-controlled school system in every city in America. I am praying that by 1990 at least 51 percent of all educable children in our country will attend a Christian private or parochial school that unashamedly teaches biblical principles for living.

3. Elect Christians to all public offices of the land. We are in a political Slough of Despond today because Christians abdicated their responsibilities to run for governmental offices a generation ago. Consequently, we have left our local, state, and federal governments in the hands of those who do not believe or practice Christian principles. It is time we realize that humanists will never legislate a moral society. Only by Christians' assuming their rightful responsibilities in government will we truly be the "salt of the earth."

4. Create a new pro-Christian television and publications network. Americans need an alternative to the anti-Christian liberalism of the present television networks. Since this is a free country, why shouldn't fifty million born-again Christians and many other millions (possibly another fifty million) have the option of tuning in a channel that will not shatter our moral sensibilities or highlight the bizarre and kinky to the exclusion of the moral and wholesome? Rather than reporting the news, our present networks "manage" it—that is, they present it from their own slanted and often biased perspective. We need an objective network that will give us the true facts about what is going on in our country and world. Our present media system so colors its presentation that Americans have not been able to vote objectively for a president in over thirty years.

5. Pray. To paraphrase Tennyson, "More things have been accomplished through prayer than this world dreams of." We need millions of people to ask God to forgive our natural sins and heal our homes. He has saved other civilizations when they turned to Him. Pray for America—there is still time for God to salvage our nation's moral decline, but it will only come in response to prayer and dedicated work on the part of every believer.

6. The church should take the lead in family-life training based on biblical principles.   The church is the best-equipped institution of our day to train today's family in the principles that produce a happy and productive homelife—for the church bases its teaching on the timeless Word of God, which is the best manual on home behavior ever devised. Although the President should be commended for appointing a commission on the family, unfortunately he neglected to appoint to that group representatives of the church who could insure its effectiveness. To fill this void, the church should become more aggressive in training its people in Christian family principles. This subject could be effectively used to bring into the church for such training the unsaved in the community who are concerned about family life. We have seen many such families come to Christ through such family-life training.

3

The Key to a Happy Marriage

All married people desire a happy marriage. Of the 439 couples for whom I have performed wedding ceremonies, not one of them asked to be married because they at last had found the one person who could make them miserable the rest of their lives. Universally, mankind has expected matrimony to usher in that fictitious refrain, "And they lived happily ever after." A quick look at the divorce statistics cited in the last chapter will verify that wedlock is realistically a calculated risk. But we are writing this book to say it *can* be a happily-ever-after experience. With God's power and your cooperation, marriage can become a miniature heaven on earth.

We pause here in our book on the family to focus upon a happy marriage—because you can't have one without the other. A couple with unresolved conflicts may beget several children, but they cannot be good parents unless they get along well together. There is no such thing as a happy family without a happy marriage.

While rummaging through over fifty books in preparation for this project, we have noted a variety of keys to a happy marriage as suggested by numerous authors. In my book *How to Be Happy Though Married* I offer "six keys" which I have organized into a basic lecture for our seminars. As important as all these keys are, one takes precedence for Christians—the same one that changed our lives and forms the heart of this book. Very simply stated, it is the filling of the Holy Spirit, or the control of the Holy Spirit.

In my years of pastoral counseling I have conferred with over 2,500 couples in the throes of marital disharmony. Not once have I had to administer such counseling to a Spirit-controlled couple. On several occasions I have pointed out the difficulty only to be told, "We used to live like that," and then hear one partner admit, "And we didn't have these problems in those days either." Very frankly, in our church counseling program we spend little time on symptoms and problems; instead we concentrate on the Spirit-controlled life. For we have found that if a couple walks in the Spirit, they can both live with or resolve their problems. If they refuse to walk in the Spirit, all the counseling on problem areas and symptoms can be likened to a doctor putting a Band-Aid on a broken leg.

Married couples need to follow three principles: (1) seek biblical instruction; (2) submit to the power of the Holy Spirit who will enable them to obey what the Bible teaches about their problem; and (3) adopt a willingness to do what the Bible says. When we find all three elements in a counselee, success is inevitable. When only two appear, we *may* see some improvement. Less than two always ends in failure. Bev and I would like to help you in the next few chapters glean the biblical instruction that has transformed our marriage. The Holy Spirit is more than willing to empower and beautify your life; the third step is entirely up to you.

The Fruit of the Spirit

"But the fruit of the Spirit is love, joy, peace, longsuffering, gentleness, goodness, faith, meekness, temperance . . ." (Galatians 5:22, 23). It is impossible for a Christian to be filled with the Holy Spirit and not evidence it in some manner. In fact, one of our fundamental presuppositions is this: "When a natural human being is filled with the supernatural power of God's Holy Spirit, he will be different!" As we have pointed out in our books on temperament (*see* Bibliography), a Spirit-controlled individual's temperament will not change but will be modified or improved, for his weaknesses will be overcome by the Holy Spirit's power. After carefully studying the forty most common weaknesses of human beings (ten for each temperament), we are thoroughly convinced that the Holy Spirit provides a strength for every human weakness. Examine the above nine "fruits" or strengths of the Spirit and you will find one sufficient to overcome every single weakness in your life. Nothing is more practical on a day-to-day basis than the control of our lives by God's Holy Spirit.

As a married woman, do you think you could get excited about going to the door at 5:30 P.M. (or whenever your husband arrives home from work) if you know that when he opens it, you will be confronted with a man who, in spite of the day's pressures and ordeals, is filled with *love, joy, peace, longsuffering, gentleness, meekness,* and so on? One wife who heard me ask that question replied, "Excited? I'd probably run to the door dressed in boots, apron, and Saran Wrap as Marabel Morgan suggests!"

As a husband, do you think you could get excited about 5:30 P.M., as you drove into the driveway, if you knew that—no matter how pressured with babies, broken appliances, and telephone interruptions your wife had been all day—when you opened the door you would discover a

woman filled with *love, joy, peace, longsuffering* . . . ?
What a marital switch that would be from the usual married
man of five years or more who is mentally exhausted at the
close of the day. Instead of driving home in the control of
the Spirit, he is still nursing grudges, fueling a cauldron of
resentment, or wallowing in the spirit of self-pity—all of
which wring out and exhaust him by the time he reaches his
front door.

The Spirit-Filled Life and Family Living

Wherefore be ye not unwise, but understanding what
the will of the Lord is. And be not drunk with wine,
wherein is excess; but be filled with the Spirit.

Ephesians 5:17, 18

The above verse provides the most specific command in
the Bible related to being filled with the Holy Spirit. Just as
a drunk is continually governed by alcohol, the wise Christian will be controlled by the Holy Spirit. Of particular
interest, this same passage contains the most extensive instruction on family living to be found in the entire New
Testament. That is why we maintain that the Spirit-filled life
is geared to family living, not primarily church activity. For
example, note the structure of the passage:

5:18	The command to be controlled by the Spirit
5:19, 20	The three results of the Spirit-controlled life
5:22–24	Wives are commanded to submit to their husbands
5:25–33	Husbands are commanded to love their wives sacrificially
6:1–3	Children are commanded to obey their parents

6:4 Fathers are commanded to nuture their children

When a Christian family is controlled by the Holy Spirit of God, the wife will submit to her husband, he will love her, the children will obey their parents, and the father will take the time to nuture his children in the Lord. Can you imagine a family that lives like that being miserable? Impossible! That is why we have never counseled a Spirit-filled couple. Clearly, the Spirit-controlled life is the real key to exciting family living.

We will highlight other aspects of Spirit-controlled Christians in later chapters, but at this point it is important to see that the true test of our being filled with the Spirit is how we live at home, not what we do away from the home. If we can live the Spirit-controlled life at home, we can live it anywhere. The pressures that mount in family living certainly surpass any we encounter elsewhere.

One lady misunderstood this fact and inadvertently admitted it when she enthusiastically exclaimed, ''I just love coming to this church! I can really feel the warmth of the Spirit of God here. Unfortunately, I don't get that feeling at home. My husband and I are having such conflict that it's impossible for me to be filled with the Spirit there!'' Very gently, I acquainted that dear sister with the truth that she was deceiving herself. If she were submitting to her husband, she could easily walk in the Spirit at home, whether or not he was obedient and showed love for her. She could enjoy church because she was free from the home's pressure-cooker atmosphere, where her rebellion against God and her husband continually confronted her. In her case, she was obedient to God in most things outside the home, so she could walk in the Spirit there; but at home she was in defiance of God and her husband. Consequently, mastery by the Spirit was impossible. When she faced her lack of submission as the hindrance to being controlled by the Spirit—so she could manifest love, joy, peace, and so on—she quit thinking about the sins of her husband, began to face her own sin of rebellion, and went home controlled by the Spirit. Her husband couldn't believe the change in his wife, and in a few weeks he too experienced the filling of the Spirit. As you can imagine, it has transformed their home.

How to Be Controlled by the Spirit

Today there is a good deal of unnecessary confusion about the filling or control of the Holy Spirit. Some theologically oriented ministers have made it so mysterious and complex that the average person can neither understand nor enjoy the experience. Other experience-oriented people tell their story with such animation and excitement that the rest of us feel rather inadequate because ours wasn't nearly that thrilling. Besides, they are relating a personal reaction which reflects the temperament and expectations of an individual. For that reason it is more profitable to look into the Word of God and seek the Bible's teachings, shunning both preconceived ideas and the personal experiences of others.

Surprisingly enough, it is really not difficult to be filled with the Spirit if you are a Christian. (It is impossible, of course, if you're not.) God does not make His commands arduous, nor do we have to beg Him to permit something He has ordered us to do. We do have to meet His conditions, however, and the major condition to being filled or controlled with the Spirit is complete surrender to His will. In its simplest form, being filled with the Spirit is a matter of obedience to every decree of God. That is why Spirit-controlled Christians can always be expected to obey the Bible. It is the clearest revelation of God's will. No one can establish a set pattern for implementing the Spirit-controlled life. However, we have shared the following three simple steps with many people. Hopefully, they will prove helpful to you as well.

1. Examine your life for sin and confess it (1 John 1:9). The Psalmist teaches us that if we harbor sin in our heart, the Lord will not hear our prayer (Psalms 66:18). Thus it is important to begin with the confession of all known sin. No one can be filled with the Spirit if he tenaciously clings to a sin habit he is unwilling to forsake.

2. Surrender your will completely to God (Romans 6:11). Once cleansed of all known sin, you should tell God formally that you are 100 percent His—that is, you are willing to do anything He instructs you to do. A procedure we have found helpful in this regard is for a person prayerfully to visualize himself lying on an Old Testament sacrificial altar. In your mind's eye picture yourself as a voluntary sacrifice, much as Abraham was about to offer his son Isaac. In this formal dedication you are affirming, "Oh, Lord, I am fully yielded to Your control. I relinquish my mind, talents, family, vocation, money, and future. Please use me to Your glory." It is a very simple procedure but extremely effective. Be sure to include in particular whatever the Lord has been speaking to you about—your temper, fears, thought life, and ambitions.

3. Ask to be controlled by the Holy Spirit (Luke 11:13). Now that you have met the conditions for being filled with the Holy Spirit, simply ask Him to fill you. Our Lord Jesus admonished us, "If ye then, being evil, know how to give good gifts unto your children: how much more shall your heavenly Father give the Holy Spirit to them that ask him?''

Many folks have written through the years to tell me how helpful is this suggestion for being filled with God's Spirit. But occasionally, theologians will try to convince me that Christ's promise was given in a different dispensation and therefore not relevant today. In so doing they reveal that they have missed the point of our Lord's observation—that God is more anxious to impart His Holy Spirit to His children than we parents are to give good gifts to ours. I realize that the promise was given prior to our Lord's experience upon the cross and before the Holy Spirit descended at Pentecost and filled the disciples. The point, however, is that what the disciples needed was the Holy Spirit, and they were taught to ask for Him. The Holy Spirit already indwells us, for we were baptized into Jesus Christ at conversion (1 Corinthians 12:13). But when we are not *filled* with the Holy Spirit, we can be filled by the same means the disciples used—by asking.

Frequently someone inquires at the close of a seminar, "How often should I ask to be filled with the Spirit?" We always reply, "Whenever you think you're not!" If you think you may have grieved Him, ask for the filling of the Spirit the first thing in the morning, several times during the day, and then at night as you drift off to sleep. After a while it gets to be a part of your life, just like breathing.

How to Walk in the Spirit

"And be not drunk with wine, wherein is excess; but be filled with the Spirit" (Ephesians 5:18)—". . . Walk in the Spirit, and ye shall not fulfil the lusts of the flesh" (Galatians 5:16). You may ask, "What is the difference between 'walking in the Spirit' and 'being filled with the Spirit'?" Actually, one is the outgrowth of the other. You cannot "walk in the Spirit" or live in the control of the Spirit on a daily basis until you are "filled with the Spirit." The experience is akin to filling yourself with water—then walking in the energy of that life-giving water. Eventually you will need to drink more so your body will have sufficient fluid to *walk* farther—and so it is with the Spirit. You will need many fillings of the Spirit in order to walk continually in His control. The following three steps for walking in the Spirit are highly practical principles found in the Scripture.

1. Develop a daily practice of reading the Word of God (Psalms 1:1–3). The Word of God is to a person what gasoline is to a car; without it the most expensive machine in the world will not operate. We have two Spirits within us—our own natural spirit called "the flesh," and the new nature called "the Spirit." The one we feed the most is the one which controls us. We do not believe it is possible for a Christian to walk in the Spirit unless he develops the habit of regularly reading the Word to nurture his *Spirit*ual nature. That is where he gains the *Spirit*ual strength to walk in the Spirit. He also is given insight into the ways of God by reading the Word.

If you have experienced a difficult time being consistent in Bible study, I have a suggestion for you. Forgive the reference to another of my books, but one of them is a very practical tool I wrote for the San Diego Chargers when I taught their weekly Bible class in our home. Several of them had faced the problem of inconsistency in their daily Bible study, so I developed *How to Study the Bible for Yourself,* a practical guide including nine different charts to aid in Bible study. Many men have found it a help in producing consistency.

2. Develop a keen sensitivity to sin (1 Thessalonians 4:3– 8). Sin is extremely subtle and will keep you from walking in the Spirit. The Scripture teaches that God has called us to holiness. Since the Holy Spirit will never lead you in the ways of uncleanness, whenever you become aware that you have begun thinking or practicing sin, you can be sure it was your *flesh* nature, not your *Spirit* nature, that led or controlled you. As you walk in the Spirit, you will gradually become sensitive to sin and avoid it.

3. Avoid quenching or grieving the Spirit (Ephesians 4:30–32).   Certain sins grieve the Holy Spirit or stifle His filling of our lives, of which anger and fear in their many forms are the most common. These, along with their remedy, will be dealt with in detail in the next chapter. Here we will merely point out that a Spirit-controlled Christian will learn to so value the *love, joy,* and *peace* which the Holy Spirit brings into His life that he will be watchful lest he grieve Him by the common emotion of anger or quench Him by the equally prevalent emotion of fear.

4

The Six Major Problems in Marriage

The Bible teaches that there are no life testings which are not "common to man." Modern psychology and popular conception would have us believe that each of us, like a snowflake, is singular. Accordingly, many people judge their problem of sin to be unique. My counseling experience, however, has substantiated the teaching of Scripture that sin is "common to man" (1 Corinthians 10:13). There are six basic enemies of marriage and the home. Fortunately, most people are not encumbered with all six. In addition, you can rejoice because the Holy Spirit can cure all of them—if you cooperate with Him.

Have you seriously reflected upon our major premise that "when a natural human being is filled with the supernatural Holy Spirit, he will be different"? Where will that difference occur? His filling certainly doesn't make us any better looking, nor does He impart more talents or a greater I.Q. He will, however, enable us to use our capabilities to their ultimate potential so that in some cases it may appear that He has given new talents to an individual. In reality, He has freed a prisoner from something that had inhibited him all his life.

One of our friends never took a piano lesson, yet he plays the organ and piano beautifully. He cannot read a note of music, but if you sing or play a song for him one time, he can reproduce it. He feels that he was given this gift when he was filled with the Holy Spirit. Actually, he was born with the ability to play music "by ear," but—because he is a sensitive and somewhat timid person by nature—his early life fears had so imprisoned him that he never seriously attempted to play a musical instrument. But, after being filled with the Holy Spirit, his natural fears were removed and he became the recipient of that "song in his heart" which we described in the last chapter. In a moment of uninhibited joy, he sat at the piano and, to his own amazement, played a little tune. With practice he has refined that skill until he is most enjoyable to listen to. In fact, he has a particular "feel" about his music that many sight readers lack. The healing of his emotions made him a whole person—and set his music ability free.

Essentially that is what the Holy Spirit does in a practical sense to each of us when we are filled with Him: He heals our emotions. That is far more significant and relevant for everyday living than most folks realize. What we are emotionally is what we are! A man may boast an I.Q. of 165, but if he loses emotional mastery, he destroys the effectiveness of his potential. It is safe to say that one's capacity to live up to his potential in life is dependent on his control of his emotions. I have found in counseling that many a severely distraught soul was both gifted and brilliant but could not pull his life together because of lack of emotional control.

Examine the twelve results or fruits which the Holy Spirit brings into our lives when we are filled with Him. "A song in your heart," "a thanksgiving spirit," and "a submissive attitude" are all emotional responses, as are the other nine fruits—*love, joy, peace* . . . . We associate these good feelings with the heart, and rightly so. Scientists refer to that "heart" as the emotional center of man. The diagram on the following page shows how the heart center is neurologically tied in with the vital organs of the body. Prolonged emotional disorders in the emotional center will eventually take a toll on some part of the body—usually the weakest point. That is what we mean by "emotionally induced illness."

S. I. McMillen, M.D., wrote an excellent book, *None of These Diseases*, from which I took the diagram. In it he listed fifty-one diseases which people can bring upon themselves due to an emotional upset. Every Christian who reads that book will understand what doctors mean when they say that 65 to 80 percent of all illness is emotionally induced. That is, the patient had nothing really wrong with him, but his emotional disturbance had brought on some ailment. Let's face it—the human body can only stand so much stress before it breaks down at its point of least resistance.

In Columbus, Ohio, I spoke on the Holy Spirit's cure for hostility in the home and listed some of the diseases I had seen Christians incur unnecessarily through protracted anger. A young internist came to me registering an interest in what I had taught. He explained that he was a specialist who received patients only on referrals from other doctors in order to diagnose difficult maladies. Then he said, "As you spoke, I began to think about the five patients I saw yesterday afternoon. All of them were angry people."

Emotions have far more control over our lives than any of us realize, and the Holy Spirit wants to cure us. You might as well let Him—before these emotions ruin your homelife as well as your body, the two most precious assets you own. It is staggering when one tries to imagine how many days a year Christians lie in hospital beds, how many

SELF-CENTEREDNESS   ENVY   JEALOUSY   RESENTMENT

HATE   WORRY   OVERSENSITIVITY   GUILT FEELINGS

FEAR   SORROW   DESIRE FOR APPROVAL   FRUSTRATION

EMOTIONAL CENTER

BRAIN

THYROID

ESOPHAGUS

LUNG

HEART

LIVER

KIDNEY

GALL BLADDER

STOMACH

UPPER COLON

ULCERS OF STOMACH AND INTESTINE   COLITIS

HIGH BLOOD PRESSURE   HEART TROUBLE   STROKES

ARTERIOSCLEROSIS   KIDNEY DISEASE   HEADACHES

MENTAL DISTURBANCES   GOITER   DIABETES   ARTHRITIS

Effects of Emotions on Physical Health

pastoral hours are spent on hospital calls, and how many millions of dollars are wasted by God's people in the considerable "unnecessary illness" category. We could probably build all the new churches and additions to the old ones needed this year with these medical expenses, if all those believers would be filled with the Holy Spirit. But that is nothing in comparison to the happiness it would engender for the homes those Christians represent. Nothing turns young people away from Christ and His church faster than emotionally upset Christian parents. They don't expect Christian parents to be perfect, but they do look for them to be controlled emotionally—and that is a reasonable expectation. When parents are filled with the Holy Spirit, they will fulfill that expectation in the home.

Emotional Conflicts—The Cause of Marital Distress

Most couples return from the honeymoon madly in love. They continue that way until they experience their first emotional conflict or clash of wills. We call this "a lovers' quarrel." Usually it isn't fatal, though it leaves a slight scar on their relationship. But making up is such fun! And they hurry down the marital path for another period of time until their next emotional eruption, followed by another exciting make-up session. Gradually these conflicts come closer together as the couple's wills and desires clash, and gradually they may turn their loving home into a "hell on earth." This may occur before or after the birth of the children, but it is rarely improved when the babies arrive. The causes for these nearly inevitable clashes—and the role of the Spirit-controlled life to heal them and their causes—form the core of this chapter.

No one has to tell a married couple that men and women are different. They are not only built differently but think, feel, and respond differently. Some of that dissimilarity is due to their sexual identity, in spite of what some unisex advocates would have us believe. But much of it is due to their opposite temperaments.

Why You Act the Way You Do

It is tempting at this point to launch into a presentation of the fascinating subject of the four temperaments, but since we have so thoroughly described them in five of our previous books (*see* Bibliography), we shall resist that temptation. It is, however, extremely valuable for the reader to know about human temperament as the best explanation to date of why people act the way they do. Many couples have found it helpful in understanding and accepting their partners, not to mention how it clarifies the reason for their own behavior.

THE FOUR BASIC TEMPERAMENTS

Super Extraverts	Ordinary Extraverts	Ordinary Introverts	Super Introverts
Sparky Sanguine	Rocky Choleric	Martin Melancholy	Phil Phlegmatic
Sarah Sanguine	Clara Choleric	Martha Melancholy	Polly Phlegmatic

We do not have space in this book to delineate the strengths and weaknesses of each of the temperaments shown. Perhaps you are already familiar with them from our other writings. It is important to point out, however, that our strengths produce our talents and desirable characteristics, whereas our weaknesses provide the inhibiting areas of our lives that often make us undesirable. It is these weaknesses which are strengthened by the power of God when we are controlled by His Holy Spirit.

Eleven years ago I wrote in *Spirit-Controlled Temperament* that a strength in the Spirit-filled life can be found for every natural weakness. At least three thousand counseling interviews later, I am even more convinced of that fact than I was then.

It has been our observation that opposites attract each other in marriage—not just sexual opposites, but contrast-

OPPOSITES ATTRACT IN MARRIAGE

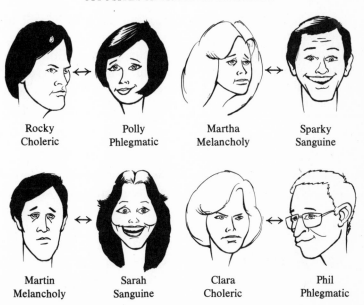

Rocky	Polly	Martha	Sparky
Choleric	Phlegmatic	Melancholy	Sanguine

Martin	Sarah	Clara	Phil
Melancholy	Sanguine	Choleric	Phlegmatic

ing temperaments. Of the four basic temperaments, it usually happens (though certainly not always) that one of the two extroverts is attracted to one of the introverts.

It is important to realize that this rule of thumb is not inviolable, and certainly in the days when parents selected partners for their children (as they still do in many places of the world), no consideration was given to temperaments. But when individuals make their own selection of a partner, we find that opposites generally attract. The reason is very subtle. We all admire others who are strong in areas in which we ourselves are weak. That admiration, under the right circumstance, often leads to love and the marriage altar. But an unsuspecting couple learns soon after the honeymoon that the partner isn't perfect after all. And, even worse, he or she is often weak in areas of the other's strengths. The temptation at that point is to look disdainfully or contemptuously upon a partner's weaknesses—or clash with them.

It is imperative that each individual learn to accept his partner's weaknesses along with his strengths and stop aggravating, criticizing, or trying to change him. God alone, with the cooperation of the individual, is able to bring about the desired change. Acceptance of the total person, whether or not you like some of his weaknesses, is essential. Detailed suggestions on how to accept and live with your partner are given in *Understanding the Male Temperament*. For our purposes here we shall clarify how the six most common emotional problems in marriage are often in conflict, depending on the partner's temperament. We shall also share a biblical technique for overcoming that weakness which is very practical and has been field-tested in our own lives and those of hundreds of others. The power to overcome these weaknesses, of course, emanates from the Holy Spirit.

The Six Emotional Problems of Marriage

THE PROBLEM OF ANGER, HOSTILITY, AND BITTERNESS

Over 80 percent of today's marriages show a predisposition to problems of anger. As one famous marriage counselor told me privately, "Whenever I am at a loss in diagnosing the cause of marital or personal problems, I always look for anger; eighty percent of the time I'm right." We had come to the same conclusion because of the fact that three of the temperaments reflect a predisposition to anger. They express it in different forms, but it is anger nonetheless. Sanguines display a quick, hot temper but immediately forget about it after their explosion. Cholerics possess an equally turbulent disposition but they can carry a grudge indefinitely and burst into flame all over again whenever reminded of what set them off. Melancholies, who are rarely quick-tempered, frequently indulge in revenge. Consequently, they mull things over for a long time, seething inwardly, but may or may not explode. Their pent-up emotions will distinctly inhibit their actual feelings and judgment. Phlegmatics rarely experience anger unless their secondary temperament is sufficiently strong to ignite them. (Everyone has two temperaments—a dominant one and a secondary one—and recent temperament tests indicate that many have three temperaments.) Consequently, many Phlegmatics do occasionally experience anger, due to their secondary temperament.

When we speak of anger, we include its various forms of bitterness, revenge, resentment, attack, and perhaps ten other expressions of hostility. In our opinion, nothing is more devastating to a marriage relationship, and no other emotion spoils family living or destroys the psyche of children, as does anger. The home was meant to be an emotional haven of peace, love, and joy to which couples and their eventual children could resort, shielded from the hostile, selfish world outside. Unfortunately, many find more hostility and animosity in their homes than on the outside.

Anger is a subtle force which circulates through many people who aren't even aware of its influence. I think of a wife who complained, "I have lost all feeling for my husband." Whenever I hear that lament, I probe for the spouse's trait or habit which upsets her, and it usually does not take long to expose it. In this woman's case it was his refusal to buy her a $58.95 garbage disposal. When he added insult to injury by saying, "My mother never had a garbage disposal, and I don't see why you need one," she became infuriated. In a matter of weeks her feeling for him had vanished. This woman was a Sunday-school department superintendent and a dedicated Christian wife and mother, but she did not realize that love and hate despise one another's company. Doubtless this is the reason the Bible so pointedly commands, "Husbands, love your wives, and be not bitter against them" (Colossians 3:19). In other words, bitterness *or* love may be expressed, but a relationship cannot admit both simultaneously. This woman confessed her sin of anger, experienced the Spirit-filled life in my office, and went home to love her husband. He could cope with her anger, but all that love finally got to him. One Saturday morning three weeks later, he surprised her with a garbage disposal.

One of the most alarming cases of anger I have ever dealt with concerned a young Christian mother who was having flashes of resentment toward her three-week-old baby. She had experienced no such feelings toward her first two little girls, but she tearfully lamented, "I think I am losing my mind and am afraid I might lose control and do something to hurt my son."

It only took a few questions to uncover a bitter, hostile spirit toward her father—who had been dead for five years. Rather than losing her mind, that woman was letting her pent-up anger construct an emotional current of hatred that was short-circuiting her normal love feelings. All it took to straighten her out was repentance of her sin of anger and the control of her mind by the Holy Spirit, so that she no longer dwelt on her father's rejection, abuse, and attempt to molest her. Had she not been able to change her thinking pattern through the Spirit's power, her father would have hounded her from his grave into an emotional breakdown or worse. Such needless tragedies occur every day.

We have dealt repeatedly with people whose inner anger, whether expressed or internalized, has caused such unnecessary tragedies as impotence, frigidity, loss of love, colitis, heart trouble, strokes, emotional breakdowns, and almost every conceivable malady common to man. If you are a regular reader of my books, you probably think I am a bit paranoid about anger because I mention it so frequently—and you may be right. The reason is that I have witnessed countless cases where it single-handedly destroyed health, love, family, children, vocations, and spiritual potential. Very honestly, another reason is that anger came so close to destroying my own family, ministry, and health. Praise God there is a remedy through the Spirit-filled life.

The Cure for Anger

Many people stubbornly maintain that some anger is desirable. Admittedly, Ephesians 4:26, 27 allows for righteous indignation, but with three qualifications: (1) *sin not;* (2) *let not the sun go down on your wrath;* and (3) *give no place to the devil.* That kind of righteous indignation is impersonal, for it is unselfishly felt on someone else's behalf. The type of anger most people experience, and that which causes the family disharmony we are concerned about, is selfish, pride-filled anger incurred when someone rejects, insults, or injures us.

Currently there is a tendency to offer well-meaning suggestions that we "use our anger," "control it", or "channel it into useful endeavors." As one explosive little lady suggested recently, "Express it!" She mistakenly believes that repressed anger is worse than expressed anger. Actually, expressing anger compounds the problem because it entrenches the habit pattern more deeply into the subconscious mind. Every time we do anything, it becomes easier to repeat the next time, as we transform the experience into a habit. That is particularly true of expressing detrimental emotions. Admittedly, repressed hostility can cause bleeding ulcers and the other fifty diseases Dr. McMillen mentions in his book. But there is a better remedy—cure it! Consider the following steps carefully, for they have been tested and many individuals have verified their effectiveness. You will find these steps to victory over anger similar to those for overcoming the other five emotional problems.

1. Face anger as a sin (Ephesians 4:30–32). No sin, habit, or weakness can be overcome unless the individual is willing to face it squarely as wrong! In the case of anger, confronting it as a sin repugnant to God is the first giant step toward cure. If you have any question about its being wrong, pursue a Bible study on anger. You will find over twenty-five verses that denounce it and many illustrations from Cain to Peter that condemn it (none more pathetic than Moses). Such a study will help you avoid the natural inclination to justify or excuse your anger. Such action is self-destructive, for it nullifies the possibility of cure. I have never seen a person overcome anger unless he readily admitted it as sin.

2. Confess your anger as sin (1 John 1:9). Not only do you need God's forgiveness for your anger every time it occurs, but you need to verbalize the fact that it is wrong and you wish to be rid of it. "God's ear is always attuned to the cry of the sinner," the Psalmist tells us, and He is quick to forgive.

3. Ask God to take away this habit pattern (1 John 5:14, 15). Anger is not merely a sin but a habit. Now that you are a Christian, you are no longer a slave to habit and even have a new power to overcome it. Thus, when anger occurs, acknowledge it as wrong, confess it in the name of Jesus Christ, and enjoy His cleansing. You should also ask for the removal of this habit pattern, knowing that anything you ask within His will He promises to do. Therefore you can confidently expect this awful habit to *gradually* fade away. Christians may be victims of a habit but they do not have to be its slave.

4. Ask for the filling of the Holy Spirit (Luke 11:13). Every time you sin, it is wise to make this request. Some Bible teachers believe we are automatically refilled with the Spirit the moment we confess our sin—and they may be right. But since I have yet to find a Scripture to prove that, I prefer to ask.

5. Give thanks for the source of your irritation (1 Thessalonians 5:18). It is essential that you change your thought patterns about the cause of your anger. That begins by thanking God *in* and *for* that circumstance or person (Ephesians 5:19, 20), realizing that it happened for your good (Romans 8:28)—it may not have been good in itself, but it happened *for* your good. Be sure you never permit your mind to dwell on that old cause of your anger. If you do, immediately follow this procedure all over again, ending with the giving of thanks.

6. Repeat this formula every time you get angry! Habits weren't build in a day, and they won't disappear overnight either. But as you use this formula, the incidence of anger will *gradually* melt away. In my own case, I honestly have to admit that once in a while I am still forced to confess a flash of temper, but so less frequently than sixteen years ago (about 300 percent improvement) that it is like being a different person.

A Seventy-Year-Old Case in Point

Three years after my own filling with the Holy Spirit, I was developing this formula for curing anger and began using it in the counseling room with exciting results. About that time the Lord began giving me invitations to hold meetings in other churches, where I shared these principles as I do now at seminars with an overhead projector. One of the first such meetings was held in a little church in Apache Junction, Arizona. At the close of my last message a rather forlorn-looking man came up and introduced himself as a deacon in the church. "Pastor LaHaye, I wish I had heard this message forty years ago! I have been an angry person all my life. Is a man seventy years of age too old to try that formula?" To be honest, I didn't really know; I hadn't tried it on that age as yet. So I prayed quickly for an answer and heard myself reply, "With man this is impossible, but with God *nothing* is impossible to you!" Noticing that, he perked up a bit. I added, "The Bible says, 'My God shall supply *all* your needs according to His riches in glory by Christ Jesus.' " Two or three other verses came to mind, and by the end of our discussion he walked away hopefully.

I forgot all about the experience for two years. When I

returned to another suburb of Phoenix, I spotted an elderly gentleman and his wife sitting in the evening service and somehow felt that I had met them before. When the service concluded, the man introduced himself as the deacon from Apache Junction. "I just came up to tell you these have been the two best years of my life. I am a different man—if you don't believe it, ask my wife!" I have found that to be the acid test! *What we are at home is what we really are.*

THE PROBLEM OF FEAR, WORRY, AND ANXIETY

Next to anger, the most common emotional problem to strike people, and consequently the family, is fear in its variety of forms. Fear was the initial negative emotion found in the Bible after Adam and Eve sinned. For the first time man was afraid of the God who loved and made him. Ever since then it has acted as an emotional destroyer. Dr. McMillen indicates that fear causes the same tensions that are induced by anger; consequently it is responsible for basically the same fifty-one physical ailments. The high-pressured pace of the nuclear age in which we live has accelerated the incidence of worry by increasing its causes and lessening many sources of security. The worldwide migration to cities forces man into a competitive environment that is far more conducive to fear than the old rural way of life.

Fear is not usually relegated to a single experience, but becomes a way of life. Fearful people worry about almost anything that is new and different, and some even fuss about rudimentary things that are familiar. A fearful person will inhibit himself vocationally, socially, educationally, and sexually. In addition, his family and spiritual life will suffer greatly. An associate and I were waiting to be seated at a restaurant for lunch when we watched a pathetic scene. A dignified Phlegmatic man about fifty was seated at the counter. When the waitress served his meal and he very softly informed her that it was not what he had ordered, she blew up all over him. He was humiliated and offended, but rather than make a scene, he just walked out of the restaurant. My associate turned to me and observed, "That man was my economics professor at San Diego State University." In all probability, the good doctor had married a woman who found it equally easy to cow him on every major issue in their marriage.

Everyone experiences fear when confronted by something dangerous or new, but if we let that fear keep us from doing what we should, it is out of hand. Doubtless you know people who refuse to drive a car but have had ample opportunity to learn. What is the *real* reason they do not learn? Fear. Driving obviously doesn't take much intelligence or mechanical ability, for otherwise millions of people worldwide wouldn't be such bad drivers. It does, however, take enough "nerve" (the term we use to express that which conquers natural fear) to try it. Repetition, however, usually overcomes those fears. Many of our routine activities today caused extraordinary fear the first time we tried them, but our anxiety was kept in check and we proceeded, however uncertain. The fear-prone person will not allow himself to do that which arouses fear. We have met several who were afraid to marry, others who feared a new job or venture. In the last few years I have taken up skiing, which I thoroughly enjoy. In the process I have confronted a number of folks who are afraid to try, even though the snowy slopes are crawling with four- and five-year-olds. Most of those who inhibit themselves by fear develop an ability to think up good excuses why they shouldn't do anything. Every church recognizes that a large number of its membership have never taught Sunday school or summer Bible school, participated in the visitation program, or involved themselves in any of the many programs of the local church. The real culprit (their ingenious excuses notwithstanding) is fear. More Christians fail to take advantage of witnessing opportunities because of fear than anything else. Almost every Christian I have met would love to share his faith and lead others to Christ—but fear may seal his lips.

Fear stifles conversation and communication in the home. It hampers many parents from insisting on standards and guidelines, and it occasions many family squabbles. We have watched sadly through the years as good parents made the fatal mistake of being afraid to discipline their teenage children. In fact, Bev and I have come to the conclusion that the most common mistake Christian parents of teenagers make is letting them pick their own friends. It can be fatal! All the good teaching of their young years goes down the drain when a young person selects carnal or unsaved teens as his dearest friends. Before long the Christian teen looks and acts like the one from a non-Christian home. The youth at church somehow lose all charm to the now carnal Christian, even though he grew up with them as his dearest friends. He is simply no longer on their spiritual wavelength. Tragically, many parents know the biblical principle that evil companions corrupt good morals (1 Corinthians 15:33), but they are afraid to say, "No!" "Stop!" or "Quit!" Why? Fear! Fear that their teen won't love them or will leave home. Ironically, they usually lose the very one their fear makes them try to save.

What causes people to be fear prone? Any explanation logically begins with their basic temperament. Phlegmatics are anxious worriers; Melancholies are fearful of criticism, injury, insult, and fear itself. A person who is part Melancholy and part Phlegmatic will, of course, be both fearful, worrisome, and insecure. Cholerics are rarely fearful unless they possess a high degree of Melancholy or Phlegmatic as a secondary temperament. In *Understanding the Male Temperament,* where I develop the twelve blends of temperament, I call those people CHLORMELS or CHLORSANS. The Sanguine, like the Choleric, isn't usually afraid of anything and may even be a daredevil, but he is insecure and so loves to please other people that he becomes fearful about gaining or maintaining their approval. Fully half of the temperament blends could produce a fear-prone person.

Temperament alone does not fully account for a person's fears, worries, and anxieties. It does, however, provide him with a predisposition toward mental anxiety which can be eased considerably by love, discipline, and security in the home—followed by strong spiritual growth. The same basic temperament subjected in childhood to rejection, lack of discipline, or unreasonable dominance without the aid of spiritual development will doubtless produce a fear-ridden adult. Add to this the possiblility of traumatic childhood experiences, a negative thinking pattern and several other fear-producing factors, and you have a real fear case on your hands.

Anger Versus Fear in Marriage

We have already seen that warm, personable Sanguines are often drawn in marriage to cool, rigid, perfectionist Melancholies. On the other hand, the quick, hot Choleric tends to prefer the calm, easygoing, never-get-upset Phlegmatic. Those are perfect formulas for collision and catastrophe in marriage because the fear inhibitions of one cause disagreements with the other. The fears of childhood are frequently overcome during the courtship stage through love, libido, and excitement. However, they gradually return after the honeymoon is over and the routine of daily living sets in. Within weeks or months the fears of one collide with the anger of the other. If the partners are not unusually unselfish people, their genuine love will begin to tarnish, and eventually they may deem their "incompatibility" grounds for divorce. But remember that incompatibility is a *result*—usually of fears and anger in collision. In *Understanding the Male Temperament* I discussed at length how a couple can generally adjust to each other's opposite temperaments. Here, however, I would like to show God's cure for the fear problem. For even if a husband or wife learns to adjust to the spouse's anger and fear, that will not solve the fear problem which inhibits the fearful partner in many areas of his life.

The Cure for Fear

Don't be disappointed if you find the cure for fear almost identical to the cure for anger. Both are temperament-induced tendencies which, through the circumstances of life, have turned into a deeply entrenched habit pattern. With God's help you will cure the habit of fear, worry, and anxiety the same way you cure any basic habit:

1. Face fear, worry, and anxiety as a sin (Romans 14:23).
2. Confess worry, fear, and anxiety as sin (1 John 1:9).
3. Ask God to take this habit pattern away (1 John 5:14, 15).
4. Ask for the filling of the Spirit (Luke 11:13).
5. Thank God for who and what He is and what He can supply in your life as you face this problem (1 Thessalonians 5:18).
6. Repeat this formula every time you become fearful.

Bev's Story

Since I have already acknowledged that I was the angry one in our relationship, you might almost guess that Bev had the fear problem by nature. Unlike many couples, we were filled with the Spirit the same week, so both of us began the process of change at the same time. As my sinful habit of anger was being replaced by the Holy Spirit's love, peace, and self-control, Bev's fears, worries, and insecurities were being modified by faith, peace, love, and self-control. This of course did wonders for our marriage. It also transformed Bev's ministry. Previous to being filled with the Holy Spirit she had limited her ministry to children under the the sixth grade. Although she was the best junior-department superintendent I had ever seen, she would never address adults. Gradually she began accepting speaking opportunities at women's conferences and banquets, and today she ministers dramatically to large women's groups and even mixed audiences in our Family Life Seminars. I have watched a beautiful rosebud, once confined by her own fears and anxieties, blossom out into a full-blown flower of poise, radiance, and Spirit-controlled confidence. But God still wanted to do a special work in her.

The director of a mission board wrote to thank me for writing *Spirit-Controlled Temperament,* which he said was "required reading for all our missionary trainees. There is just one problem with it. You tell how God delivered your wife from her fear of public speaking, but later admit she couldn't join you and the rest of the family in waterskiing because she was afraid of the water. The problem is that our non-swimming missionary candidates readily identify with her and use her as an excuse for not learning to swim—which could prove fatal to some of them." He went on to graciously ask, "Isn't the fear of water just as much a sin as the fear of anything else?"

I thought about that letter for two days and then took it home and asked Bev to "sit down. I have something for you to read." As she began reading, I went into the next room and got her the Kleenex box, which she needed. Several days later I heard her on the phone, talking about "swimming lessons." She cleverly lined up a heated swimming pool and a Phlegmatic instructor. Dressed in my rubber wet suit (which I wear in the winter for waterskiing—it not only keeps you warm but makes it impossible to drown), she also strapped on a life belt. Arming herself with her New Testament, she quoted: "I will never leave you or forsake you," and other verses on assurance of God's provision. Eventually she was able to discard the unnecessary paraphernalia and learned to·swim. She will never be a U.S. Olympic candidate but she conquered her terrible fear of water.

Last summer while the family was enjoying our annual waterskiing trip at Lake Powell, I stood on the back of our rented houseboat, looking down at her swimming in water 175-feet deep and thinking, "Who but Jesus Christ, by His Holy Spirit could replace obsessive fear with relaxing faith?"

THE PROBLEM OF SELFISHNESS

The number-three bomb in the arsenal of marriage problems is basic to all mankind—selfishness. We are all born with it, and to one degree or another it plagues us throughout life. In our opinion, one of the chief responsibilities of parents is to train their children away from selfishness. Every baby comes home from the hospital with the self-centered attitude that he is the only child on earth. Any perceived need for food, sleep, or a diaper change will occasion a howl of protest: "I want attention now!" We accept that as normal because he is immature. But unless trained out of it through years of love and discipline, he will still be immature at twenty years of age and will serve as a bad risk for marriage. A candidate for matrimony should look carefully at the "unselfishness quotient" of the partner-to-be. If he is unselfish, his anger or fears will be kept in better check and any other undesirable characteristics will be more easily overlooked. The hardest person to love over a period of time is not one who is unattractive or possesses a zero personality, but a partner who is selfish.

An egocentric person thinks of himself first and foremost in everything. Consequently, he finds giving and sharing a difficult habit to cultivate. All temperaments have their own tendencies to be selfish, but some are by nature more easily trained out of them. A Sanguine is selfish about his person, for his giant ego requires that he remain the center of attention at all times. Cholerics selfishly run roughshod over others or use people for their own purposes, then cast them off when they are through. Melancholies are prone to be self-centered and evaluate everyone from the standpoint of what is good for themselves. Phlegmatics are overprotective of themselves, often afraid they will be hurt or offended, and they are apt to be stingy.

Selfishness Is a Loser

Happiness is dependent on learning to share one's self, time, talents, and possessions with others. Ideally, love overcomes selfishness during the courtship days and often through the honeymoon. But gradually a person's basic selfish habits return after that, and love dies proportionately. For that reason, money problems arise quickly in the marriage—so frequently that many counselors call this the chief difficulty in matrimonial adjustment. Methods of handling money fairly and frugally are important, but improved methods never change a selfish heart; they just make it easier to live with Mr. Selfish.

Money is only one subject which is distorted by selfishness. Others include children, parents, holidays, sports, hobbies, lovemaking, churchgoing, giving, and most other facets of living.

The Bible offers extensive comment on selfishness. Consider the following examples:

[Jesus' Golden Rule] Give unto others as you would have them give unto you.

See Matthew 5:42; 7:12

Give, and it shall be given unto you; good measure, pressed down, and shaken together, and running over, shall men give into your bosom. For with the same measure that ye mete withal it shall be measured to you again.

Luke 6:38

But whoso hath this world's good, and seeth his brother have need, and shutteth up his bowels of compassion from him, how dwelleth the love of God in him?

1 John 3:17

Let nothing be done through strife or vainglory; but in lowliness of mind let each esteem *other* better than themselves. Look not every man on his own things, but every man also on the things of *others*.

Philippians 2:3, 4

True love and giving all of oneself and one's possessions to those one loves are inseparable. Love is not static; it is an emotional motivator which causes a person to give. Love may well reside in a selfish person's heart, but it may be dammed up by self-love. As we shall see in a later chapter, our love priorities should be (1) love God supremely; (2) love our partner; and (3) love our neighbor as ourself.

The Cure for Selfishness

The same basic cure for anger and fear will work for selfishness, so I will leave it to the reader to enlarge and apply the following abbreviated steps:

1. Face selfishness as sin.
2. Confess it.
3. Ask God to take away this habit.
4. Ask for the filling of the Spirit.
5. Thank God for His love that is flowing through you to make you a more generous person.
6. Repeat this formula each time you do, say, or *think* anything that is selfish.

Gradually this habit pattern will begin to fade, and a mature generosity and true love for others will replace it. Your patience toward others will also be extended; you will increasingly enjoy others and they will begin enjoying you. Philippians 2:3, 4, cited above, emphasizes the words *other* and *others*. A mature, unselfish, person never lacks for friends, for he is so "others" conscious that they recognize it and feel comfortable in his presence. In the family, such a person is a delight to have around the house. Instead of being interested in his own rights or possessions, he develops "others" awareness.

The Problem of Infidelity

Since earliest times the misuse of man's God-given sex drive has proven to be a major human problem. The Holy Spirit was obviously aware of that fact, for in His list of seventeen common "works of the flesh" (Galatians 5:19–21) the first four are sexual sins: adultery, fornication, uncleanness, lasciviousness. They were problems in Israel, the Corinthian church was plagued with them, and rampant sexual vice is predicted for the last days. If we are indeed in the last days, we can expect the appetite for immorality to increase.

In the early days of our ministry we occasionally were

confronted by all kinds of unfaithfulness among couples—from incest to homosexuality and back through all conceivable forms of fornication—even among church families. For reasons already given, the forms of temptation have increased, and the number of Christians falling into these sins has risen alarmingly. On many occasions we have been brought in to help pick up the pieces of people's lives destroyed by such infidelity. God's grace is sufficient to put things back together, but immorality usually leaves scars that only years of faithfulness can erase.

God's plan has always designed one man for one woman, as long as they both live. Anything short of that is a sin against God and a betrayal of the trust of your dearest friend. Faithful partners, we may add, are not untempted partners. Almost every red-blooded person has had opportunity to cheat on his mate, but love, honor, and duty rejected the possibility. You don't accrue any brownie points for such action, but you escape the impending load of guilt and shame it causes. We have counseled many couples six months or a year after their sin and found that it occasioned sexual maladjustment problems not experienced previously. The wages of all sin are much too high—and that is particularly true of sexual sins.

The Cure for Infidelity

For two reasons, the practice of immorality, interestingly enough, is easier to break than the emotional sins cited earlier. First, it is so blatantly sinful that only an extremely strong-willed, carnal Christian denies it is sin (after he gets caught). Although in the last few years some Christians have actually tried to tell me they were Spirit-filled while living away from their wife and with another woman, most Christians recognize such activity as sin. Self-deception is simply the result of a long sin pattern. Second, it is easier to

gain victory over sexual than emotional sins because no
habit pattern is involved. Sexuality is a physical function
that takes two people. But the pattern of mental-attitude
lust must be cured before lasting victory can be obtained—
and that is a habit.

Our Lord was always perceptive of human nature when
He spoke (". . . for he knew what was in man" [John
2:25]), but never more so than when He said,
". . . whosoever looketh on a woman to lust after her has
committed adultery with her already in his heart" (Matthew
5:28). The Christian who never commits mental-attitude
lust will never commit adultery! Even though the secular
world of psychology commonly suggests that sexual fantasies are normal (the everyone's-doing-it routine), they are
wrong. This premise lies in direct conflict with the teaching
of Jesus Christ. As one of the Scriptures already quoted
about the Holy Spirit teaches: "For God hath not called us
unto uncleanness, but unto holiness" (1 Thessalonians
4:7)—and this begins in the mind.

The people of Noah's day were sexual degenerates whom
God destroyed. ". . . every imagination of the thoughts of
his heart was only evil continually" (Genesis 6:5). Such
thought patterns are easily ignited today by the increase of
pornography, X-rated movies, and so on, but no Christian
man or woman has to be in bondage to such sin. He that is
in us is greater than he that is in the world. Therefore we
need not become slaves to sin. In addition, it is almost
unnecessary to add that no one whose mind is filled with
lustful thoughts can be filled with the Holy Spirit. The following six steps to overcoming infidelity—or the adulterous
lust thoughts that produce it—will provide a cure, *before*
those thoughts inspire the intense feelings that lead to the
marriage-jolting sin:

1. Admit that all lust thoughts and adultery are sin (Matthew 5:28).
2. Confess them each time they occur (1 John 1:9).
3. Ask God to take away the pattern and cleanse your mind (1 John 5:14, 15).
4. Ask for the filling of the Spirit (Luke 11:13).
5. Thank God for His victory and concentrate on pure thoughts (Philippians 4:8).
6. Repeat this formula each time you indulge lustful thoughts.

Doctors of the mind and students of human nature tell us that twenty-one days of abstinence will break a habit. I tried it on coffee one time, assuming they were right (to prove to myself I could break the habit), then returned to it on the twenty-second day, because I enjoy the taste. Their prescription may work for habits, but personally I think it takes longer than that when we attempt to train the mind or control our thoughts. It is verified in 2 Corinthians 10:5 that we *can* bring our thoughts into obedience to Christ. In the case of one who has been practicing the habit of mental-fantasy lust for a long time, the frontal lobe of his brain (the thinking, reasoning, and remembering bank) is saturated with lustful thoughts in living color. It will take at least three to four months of pure-thinking days to force those memories (even if only fantasies) to recede to a less influential part of the mind.

One man I worked with for over a year fought an intense battle with lust. He finally cured his problem by fining himself each time he regressed. His self-chosen fine was to memorize a verse of Scripture. The last time I talked to him, he was reviewing a packet of 129 Scripture cards. Why was he victorious? Because he meant business.

Married Lovemaking

The Bible clearly teaches that one of the major purposes for the act of marriage is mutual pleasure and the lessening of sexual temptation. Marital lovers enjoy the intimacy, warmth, and fulfillment they share, followed by the afterglow of the sense of rightness, because it is approved of God. No clandestine "affair" can ever equal such a sexual experience. If you have difficulties or if your marital love life is not satisfying to you, we recommend our book *The Act of Marriage*.

The Problem of Self-Rejection

In recent years we have been alerted to the universal problem of self-rejection. Unlike those we have already discussed, this emotion is not always readily apparent. Instead, it may be so deeply internalized that it goes unrecognized—because it adopts so many faces, which vary with the individual and the occasion. Self-rejection can cause a person to retreat socially and vocationally, check the expression of his personality, indulge in self-depreciation, concede his inferiority, fall into depression, or succumb to a host of other misconceptions, some even quite bizarre. At best, it incites capable people to sell themselves short in life.

There are many causes for self-rejection, including temperament, but the most important are parental disapproval, criticism, and rejection. Usually the child who is given love and warmth in the home, particularly during the early stages of life, does not have a problem with self-rejection unless he has a strong Melancholy temperament. One of the weaknesses of the Melancholy is his spirit of criticism, which he often uses on himself. The Holy Spirit-filled life is the only remedy for this.

In *How to Win Over Depression*, I go into detail on this

subject, so I will not belabor the point here, except to list the general causes and cure. Most people reject their appearance, talents, environment, parents, or future. Few reject all five. If they do, of course, they are in serious trouble. Those who have read our books may add one more area of rejection—their temperament. Regardless of the temperament combination they possess, they are certain that they would be happy had they been something else. Actually, as I have noted on several occasions in print or in public, no one temperament or combination of temperaments is better than another—though some are better than others *for certain things.* For example, I don't think I would go to Dr. Sanguine if I thought I had something seriously wrong with me. As a pilot I might see him for a quick medical exam to satisfy the F.A.A., but if I were suspicious that I had a serious ailment, I would see Dr. Melancholy or Dr. Phlegmatic. (Dr. Choleric is usually too rough. By the time he gets through probing or jabbing the tender area, the problem has gotten worse. He is excellent, however, during wartime as a battlefield doctor, or as supervisor of the emergency ward in some big hospital—if he doesn't have to make too many snap decisions.)

The Cure for Self-Rejection

The self-rejecting individual must first come to realize that he is in defiance of God. When we dislike our looks, body size, temperament, or talent, who do we blame? God, of course. He is the One who arranged at conception the genes that produced us. Many people have said or implied, "I don't care what you say; if God loved me He would not have made me this way." Such thinking is not only sinful but will lead to sickness, thus compounding the problem. Only by facing their ingratitude, unbelief, and rebellion against God will such individuals learn to accept themselves. The following steps apply our method of cure to self-rejection:

1. Face and confess self-rejection as sin.
2. Ask God to take away the habit of self-rejection.
3. Ask Him for the filling of the Spirit (Luke 11:13).
4. Thank Him for who and what you are (1 Thessalonians 5:18).
5. Repeat this formula each time self-rejection occurs.
6. Look for an area to serve God and others (Romans 12:1, 2).

It is particularly important that Christian self-rejecters *formally* at least one time thank God for who and what they are. If appearance is your subject of rejection, then look at your reflection in the mirror and thank God for how you look, particularly those areas you have been rejecting. Remember, if God had wanted you to look otherwise, you would. Then thank Him for your talents and offer them to Him. Even if you consider your gifts only minimal, He is a master at taking ordinary people and doing superordinary things with them. I can certainly vouch for that. If I told you my high school and college English grades, you would probably stop reading this book immediately. If you saw my penmanship, you probably couldn't make out half the words. Our God has never been limited to talent, and since He is the Source of all power, let Him flow through you. Everyone will be amazed at the result.

You might wonder why I include self-rejection in this list of family enemies. I agree with Bill Gothard, who said, "A person's attitude toward himself will influence his attitude toward God, others, and everything he does." To function at your maximum efficiency, you must realize that you are important enough for God to let His Son die for you, and that God wants to use your life, beginning in your own home.

Many well-meaning Christians cling to the mistaken notion that self-acceptance or love for one's self is unspiritual. Admittedly, one fruit of the Spirit is "meekness," but our Lord assumed self-acceptance when He said, "Love your neighbor as yourself." God's divine order is clear—love Him supremely, then your partner and children, and finally your neighbor and yourself equally. If you depreciate yourself, it will keep you from loving your family as you should. An excellent book on this subject is James Dobson's *Hide or Seek.*

THE PROBLEM OF DEPRESSION

Fifty thousand to seventy thousand annual suicides due to depression verify the seriousness of this problem in our culture. Any Christian counselor will testify that it is one of the most common disabilities he confronts. Because many Christians refuse to seek the aid of counselors, they try to live with the pain like a low-grade infection in the body, as if it were a necessary part of life.

Depression was saved for last, not because it is the least important, but because it is a result of anger, fear, and self-rejection. The many symptoms and causes are detailed in *How to Win Over Depression* which should be helpful to those who are plagued by this enemy to happy family living, for I wish to point out that a cure *does* exist. I am convinced that no Spirit-filled Christian will be depressed. In fact, depression should serve as a warning that one is not filled with God's Spirit but permeated with self.

The problem of depression can be cured quite readily if one is willing to face what causes it. But many strike out right there. The real problem is *self-pity* (unless it is a physiological problem, which is relatively rare). Every time a person uses any of the reasons everyone offers for indulging in self-pity, he begins to get depressed. You can actually chart your own depression, for its intensity will vary with the degree of self-pity. The time sequence is also important. Usually within one to twenty-four hours after one inaugurates the process of self-pity, he becomes aware of the depression. Those who have nurtured self-pity for years (until they are quite skilled at it) may be able to feel its effects in a matter of minutes.

Depression never starts without provocation. A happy, well-adjusted person will not suddenly become depressed, as if he were hit by a viral infection. Usually he will find that something specific happened or will remember a previous unfortunate event—perhaps rejection by someone he loves, an insult, or an injury. The following depression-producing formula should be cemented in your mind. Anytime you find yourself drifting into depression, think of this formula and then follow the steps for a cure.

$$\left.\begin{array}{l}\textbf{Rejection}\\\textbf{Insult}\\\textbf{Injury}\end{array}\right\}\ \textbf{SELF-PITY = DEPRESSION}$$

The Cure for Depression

1. Face self-pity as a mental sin pattern.
2. Confess this sin of the mind.
3. Ask God to take away this thought pattern.
4. Ask for the filling of the Holy Spirit.
5. Thank God in the midst of the rejection, insult, or injury that He is with you, supplying all your need.
6. Repeat this formula each time you find yourself depressed.

The Spirit-Filled, Happy Home

At great length we have dealt with what we consider the six most prolific problem areas facing Christian families today. All of them grieve or quench the Holy Spirit and limit His use of our lives. If you find one or more of these problems cropping up in your life or family, discuss it with your partner and follow the recommended procedure for cure. Any home so filled with the Spirit that the members almost never see one of these enemies attack will enjoy a "song in the heart," a thanksgiving attitude, a submissive spirit—love, joy, peace, and all the other graces that really constitute a Christ-centered, happy home.

A Personal Note

This chapter contains several suggestions that you read some of our other books. We hope you will not take offense at this—for we certainly are not trying to be commercial. Our purpose is to help those readers who have a particular problem in an area we have previously covered in detail. What most folks don't realize about our books is that they have grown out of our experiences in counseling people, and each one was addressed to a specific problem. It so happens that these are the most common problems facing families today. We are great believers in the power of the Holy Spirit to help people through reading, for we too have been helped immeasurably by the writings of others. We also have great confidence in the power of a single decision. That is, when a man or woman faces the biggest problem area in his life as a sin, he is well on the road to recovery. In my case it was anger; in Bev's it was fear. We hope and pray that if you have a problem area that is hindering your family life, the Holy Spirit revealed it in this chapter and that you are willing to make that big decision that can revolutionize your life—face it as sin, let God cleanse you and remove this habit from your life.

5

The Roles of the Wife

The supreme hallmark of the Spirit-controlled family is not happiness, children, or prosperity. It is obedience to the Word of God. The happiness and fulfillment experienced by the Spirit-controlled family are a result of that obedience. Our Lord said, "Blessed [happy] are they that hear the Word of God, and keep it" (Luke 11:28; *see also* Psalms 119:1 and John 13:17). The two requirements for happiness are hearing the Word and keeping the Word. Based on those verses, the following formula has been developed—

$$\text{Hearing the Word of God} + \text{Keeping the Word of God} = \textbf{HAPPINESS}$$

Everyone seeks happiness on a lasting basis. It is never found, however, as the result of a quest, but as a consequence of obedience to God's Word. This is significantly true for the family. For that reason, now that we have reviewed the biblical solution to marriage's six greatest enemies, let us return to the longest New Testament text on the family (Ephesians 5:17–6:4) and examine the three results of the Spirit-controlled life: (1) a song in the heart; (2) a thanksgiving attitude; and (3) a submissive spirit (5:19–21). These results set the stage for a most significant subject: the roles of both wife and husband.

God has clearly outlined the role of the woman and the

role of the man. Just as they have complementary physical characteristics, so they enjoy complementary roles. The success of both roles demands cooperation by both partners. That is why He prefaced the role instruction with verse 21: "Submitting yourselves one to another in the fear of God." Partners who truly submit to each other have no difficulty accepting the biblical teaching on roles or subjecting themselves to them, and thus they help each other fulfill those roles.

The roles of the wife are filled with challenge to become a versatile woman. More than being a mother, lover, or helpmeet, the success-seeking young woman is assured of a multifaceted career, a challenge that few professions can offer. The circle below establishes the various roles of the wife that we will cover in this chapter.

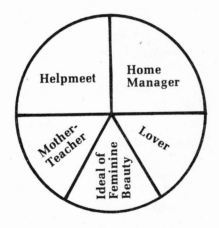

The Wife as Helpmeet or Subordinator

A "helpmeet" is one who can adequately fulfill the needs of her partner. Ephesians 5:22 NAS instructs women: "Wives, be subject to your own husbands . . ." or to submit to them. This does not mean that the woman is inferior or unequal, but that she remains under the authority of the husband. She is a subordinate, a vice-president, who serves directly under the head of the household or the president, who is the husband. Because this is God's design, she cannot be a spiritual woman without obeying the command of submission. Verse 22 follows directly from verse 18, which tells her to be filled with the Spirit. The true filling of the Holy Spirit will cause and enable a woman to submit to her husband in love.

A warning to the twentieth-century woman is in order. Do not be confused or misled by the false teaching that is sweeping our country. Outspoken women today are proclaiming that a woman should not be subordinate to her husband; she should "do her own thing" and act as a freethinker, even to the point of changing roles with the man. Such labels as NOW, ERA, or IWY purportedly grant feminist leaders the authority to speak for all American women. However, many of these feminists are not married to happy husbands, some are divorced, others are known lesbians, and few demonstrate the characteristics of "femininity." When speaking out against husbands and families, they are rebels against God. Christian women need to rise up and unanimously declare that the radical feminist protesters represent only themselves. And since much in their platform is not in accord with God's plan for womanhood, it is impossible to follow the entire program and remain Spirit-controlled women.

The Bible teaches women that their attitude toward the husband should be that of reverence, respect, and submission. "Submission" does not imply that a woman is stripped of her rights, manacled, and reduced to a "slave." On the contrary, submission allows her *more* freedom— because she is obeying the law of God and following the path of righteousness. Just as our national freedoms can only be guaranteed as we submit ourselves to the law, so a person can only be truly free when obeying God's principles. The unfortunate Women's Lib leaders who cry out for more freedom will never experience true liberation until they have first met Jesus Christ and followed His plan for women's freedom.

Submission does not mean suppression or silence; it does not incarcerate a woman in a concentration camp. To be a real helpmeet means to help by offering your thoughts, insights, and feelings. Every wife will have opinions and personal convictions on most subjects, and they may not always agree with her husband's. Submission does not involve closing her mouth, shutting off her brain, and surrendering her individuality. The loving husband who is wise will seek the insights of his wife before he makes that final decision. We have found in our own marriage that we repeatedly see things differently and frequently do not agree on how to approach difficult circumstances. Because Tim has allowed me to develop my own thoughts and feelings, thus retaining my uniqueness, he listens respectfully to my counsel and considers it carefully before making the final decision. Occasionally, I have unduly influenced him and he has made an incorrect decision. This causes me to be more cautious and to weigh my remarks carefully, being certain that they are words of wisdom, for they carry substantial weight with him. I have learned through the years that the Holy Spirit gives special wisdom to husbands who are following the pattern of a Spirit-filled man. When the wife has offered her observations and convictions, she *submits*—in committing her husband to God as he makes the final decision. She must submit even more when that decision is contrary to her own perspective. After all, there can only be one authority—one general, one president of the corporation. When the wife entrusts her husband and the decision to God, she is submitting fully and is leaving the consequences, good or bad, to her Heavenly Father. True submission is in force when her attitudes and actions are in complete agreement. It is not a matter of *pretending* to be submissive, for her genuine attitude and desire should be to submit. In addition, she is not subject to her husband because he is such a "wonderful, well-deserving person who dearly loves his wife and is consistently obedient to God." She will not protest, "I will only yield to that carnal man when he straightens out and regains sound spiritual stability." No, she submits because she wants to be obedient to God and maintain a close relationship with Him. The wife's attitudes and actions of submission are a measure or barometer of her relationship to Christ. Verse 22 charges her to be subject to her own husband *as to the Lord.* The next two verses compare the wife/husband relationship to that of the church and Christ. As the church is subject to or under the authority of Christ, so should the wife be under the authority of the husband.

Remember, the wife should not submit simply in order to reap the results in her husband. Her true obedience lies in submission as his helpmeet, leaving the change and results up to God. One woman asked, "How can I submit to my husband when he isn't obeying what God commanded him to do?" I replied, "Submission is not contingent on the actions of your partner. Leave him to the Holy Spirit."

Another woman rejected the teachings on the authority of the husband. She argued, "Why is so much said about how the woman submits and so little is required of the husband?" Because of her rebellious attitude toward God, this same woman has had difficulty in totally surrendering to Jesus Christ. She wants to play the game of life *her* way, even though she will lose. You cannot win without playing according to God's rules.

While leading a woman's Bible study one day, I was interrupted by a troubled wife who grumbled, "Why is it that the woman gets the most difficult part of the marriage relationship, that of submitting?" Before I could answer, a transformed rebel replied, "I must disagree with you. The husband has the most difficult position. He is responsible for making final decisions that affect the wife, the children, and their future. All I am required to do is submit to him and serve as a helpmeet. The blame or glory for decisions falls wholly on him." That stimulated a very lively discussion, and we concluded that God's assignments to husbands and wives were not in accord with their individual abilities, but rather with their utter dependence upon Him, thus enabling them to fulfill the roles assigned. In God's eyes their roles are balanced: "However, in the Lord, neither is woman independent of man, nor is man independent of woman" (1 Corinthians 11:11 NAS). The man is the head of the woman, but the woman is the one who gives birth to the man. One cannot function adequately without the other. The wife is told to submit to her own husband as unto the Lord. Why? Because the husband sits in the place of Christ in authority and responsibility. He is the head of the family, the image and glory of God, whereas "the woman is the glory of the man" (1 Corinthians 11:7). Neither has a simple assignment, but their roles can be fulfilled when the Holy Spirit is in control of their lives and their greatest desire is to be obedient to God.

Submission is reserved "unto your own husband." Women are not expected to be subject to men in general. Some extreme teachings have grown from this biblical injunction, including the false idea that women should be subject to all men, or that single girls should be under the authority of their single male dates. Do not misconstrue the explicit limits of this scriptural command. The wife is to respect and reverence *her own husband*. However, when a single girl is considering marriage, she should definitely ask herself whether this prospective husband is one to whom she could lovingly submit after marriage. Is he the kind of individual she could respect and reverence? Could she willingly place herself under his authority? If not, then marriage would be a great risk, for it would take place without God's blessing.

A wife loves the qualities in her husband that distinguish him from other men. She is attracted to his manhood, and part of that manliness is that he will be the leader of the home. If she refuses to submit and begins to dominate him, she will destroy that part of him that is God-designed and unique, his leadership capability. In subverting this, she is on the road to sacrificing her love and respect for that man. A woman who nags generates one of two responses in her husband: (1) he becomes stubborn, irritable, and obstinate; or (2) he just gives in to keep peace, though inside he begins to resent her and harbor bitterness in his heart. Whichever results, he becomes less than the man she envisioned when they married. Eventually, the unique manly characteristics that originally attracted her will fade from view, leaving both partners unfulfilled and unhappy.

Later in marriage the woman who has never learned submission in action and attitude wakes up to another potential problem. During the days of child raising, she dominated the children and bossed them around. When the children have grown, her increased self-confidence and dominance may then be directed toward the husband. Because her wits and skills have developed over the years, her husband may now serve as the sole target for her domination. The retirement years then become the "rough and rugged years" instead of the "rest and relaxed years." The latter period of life will be what you have been becoming together.

WHY A WIFE SHOULD SUBMIT TO HER HUSBAND

1. She will never be a Spirit-filled woman unless she does. There is no other way to become a godly woman without fulfilling the command to submit to the husband. Any other demonstrations of the Spirit-filled life will be illegitimate.

2. She presently has or will ultimately experience an emotional need to lean on a husband. Her temperament will determine whether she leans on him early in marriage or reaches that point with maturity. The Phlegmatic and Melancholy temperaments will adjust quite readily to leaning on their husbands in the early days of marriage. They normally shy away from the burden of being independent and find it comfortable to lean on their partner. However, Sanguine and Choleric women are much more independent and enjoy the role of leadership and responsibility. But even they reach the stage in life when they need to lean on the strength and security of a loving husband. How they have submitted in the early years of marriage will greatly determine how much the husband can be counted on for leaning in the latter years.

3. Her husband has a need for her to submit. This is not something the husband learns or tries to develop. It is a built-in need which God designed for him. He greatly needs to be respected and admired, just as she needs to be loved. The husband can become head of the household in two ways. One is by the wife's election. She determines in her heart that this is right and, as she submits, she "elects" him to be the authority of the home. The second way occurs when the husband demands to be the head and becomes a self-appointed dictator. The first choice, resulting from two people willing to be led by the Holy Spirit, will lead to a loving and harmonious relationship. The second choice is self-motivated, and since it does not give way to the Spirit's leading, it produces friction and resentment. A husband cannot be the loving authority of the wife unless she allows him to be through submission.

4. Their children need her submission to grow up with normal sex direction and proper role examples. The child's greatest potential for a happy, normal marriage relationship will be founded upon the example set by Mom and Dad. He can best learn at home how a husband should function as head of the family and the wife as submissive helpmeet.

SUBMITTING TO AN UNSAVED HUSBAND

The questions often arise: "Should a wife submit to an unsaved husband—and how far must she go in submission?" Large numbers of Christian women are married to unsaved husbands who have not accepted Jesus Christ as Saviour and Lord, so that is an important question to consider.

It is commanded in 1 Peter 3:1, 2: "In the same way, you wives, be submissive to your own husbands so that even if any of them are disobedient to the word, they may be won without a word by the behavior of their wives" (NAS). Is that a clear answer? "In the same way" refers back to 1 Peter 2:21–25, which establishes that Christ has been an example for us to follow. Even though we strayed like sheep, we have now returned to the Shepherd. You, dear wife, must be the example of Christ in you, exhibiting behavior and attitudes in the home that will win your husband to Christ. It will not be your words of nagging or preaching that will woo him, but your devoted behavior and your submission. When you put yourself under his authority and demonstrate honor, respect, and loving deeds, Jesus Christ will be seen more clearly in your life than any words you could ever speak. Nagging and preaching will only drive a wedge between your husband and Jesus Christ. In some homes more sermons are preached to husbands than a minister could ever deliver to his congregation. Yet these same dominant, preachy figures at home will come to church and pray publicly for their unsaved husbands. More would be accomplished if they would go home and apologize to their husbands for nagging, place themselves "under his authority," and begin to let their behavior at home speak for itself. Jesus Christ can more beautifully be seen through a changed life than through the greatest oratory in the world. If these women want to win their husbands to Christ, they need to concentrate more on their relationship to Christ and submission to their husbands than on church activities and a busy Christian social life. Their prayer should be: "Lord, change me"—prior to "Lord, save my husband." If the woman's husband is still unsaved, she must confront herself with the thought that "perhaps he has not been able to see enough of Christ in me!"

Submission is the key word. The only exception to this absolute rule is if the husband should ask her to do something that is contrary to the teachings of the Bible, such as stealing or committing adultery. Then he is no longer acting under the authority of God, who never authorizes us to do something that He has previously disallowed. For the Bible teaches that ". . . we ought to obey God rather than men" (Acts 5:29).

The Wife as Home Manager

The husband is to be the supervisor of the home, but the wife will do the actual managing. This does not mean that she will make all the decisions. Rather, she will put into operation the general policies that have already been formulated by the supervisor and the manager, including the decisions that fall within her sphere.

Norman V. Williams in *The Christian Home* refers to the origins of the two words *husband* and *wife*. The word *husband* means "house-band." He is the one who "bands" or "binds" the home together. The strength and the stability that the band must possess to hold the family together is represented by the husband. In contrast, the word *wife* means "weaver." She is the one who uses her clever hands to weave into the family fabric the beautiful designs which produce much joy and blessing.

Too often women say, "I'm just a homemaker," sensing that they may have missed something in life by following such a calling. That is one reason why we prefer to label it "home manager." The challenges are so numerous that the position should be elevated to managerial level. Our standards for home management seem to have dwindled since the example of the "virtuous woman" described in Proverbs 31. There was a day when that woman and I were not on speaking terms. In fact, I used to close my ears at the mere mention of the woman. I considered her standards far out of reach and extremely impractical. But today, perhaps after developing maturity and spiritual growth, I can clearly recognize her sterling example to all Christian women. When her functions are translated into present-day activities, they formulate a practical goal that we can set before us to frame characteristics that we can hope to attain. It certainly takes the "just" out of "just a homemaker."

Permit me the privilege of giving Proverbs 31:10–31 a LaHaye paraphrase for the twentieth-century woman.

The Twentieth-Century Woman of Proverbs

31:10   An excellent wife is hard to find. She cannot be bought with expensive jewels or fancy sports cars. Her inner beauty cannot be purchased—it is far greater than money can buy.

31:11   Her husband trusts her with all of his possessions. He is not concerned that she will drain the checkbook or run up the charge account for her own whims. Rather, she will help to save and economize in order to establish financial security.

31:12   She is a devoted helpmeet for his good, a ''responder'' to his love, one who lives for his fulfillment.

31:13   She decorates the home, keeps the house tidy, and even mops the floor with a song in her heart and praise on her lips.

31:14   She shops wisely at the local supermarket and fresh-vegetable stands for the best buys in food and provides well-balanced nutritious meals that are attractively served.

31:15   She rises early in the morning and serves a good breakfast to her husband and children before driving her children to school and starting her day's schedule.

31:16   She holds home Tupperware parties. From the money she earns, she pays her children's tuition for a Christian education.

31:17   She goes to the local health club and exercises her body to keep physically fit and strong.

31:18   She senses when her muscles are well toned,

because she can keep up with the busy pace of her family well into the evening.

31:19   She picks up her needlepoint when she sits down, and keeps her hands busy.

31:20   She makes time to assist those who are needy, making soup and casseroles for the sick neighbors and arranging time for volunteer charity work for the poor.

31:21   She is a season ahead, planning what warm winter clothes will be needed for the family before the snow begins to fall.

31:22   She selects her own wardrobe carefully and is well groomed in modest apparel. She is not seen outside her home with curlers in her hair, nor does she dress to gain attention.

31:23   Her husband is a respected businessman among the leaders of the community.

31:24   She operates a ladies' boutique from her home (some might term it a "garage sale"), selling some of the lovely articles that she has created.

31:25   Charm and self-confidence are her character istics, and she faces the future with joy and hope.

31:26   She speaks with wisdom from studying the Word of God, and her life is an example of kindness to others.

31:27   She manages her home with great care and does not sit around idly, watching TV or chatting with her friends on the telephone.

31:28   Her children love and respect her, and her husband sings her praises, saying:

31:29   "You, my darling, are the greatest woman God could have given me."

31:30   A charming and beautiful woman can be deceiving, but a woman who reveres the Lord shall be praised.

31:31 Her children and her community, who know her well, will see all that she has done and will admire and praise her.

Did you catch the theme which runs through every activity of the Proverbs woman? Her career is centered in home and family. Everything she does is to better her home and improve the family. She is the "weaver" who intertwines the different threads of the home to produce the beautiful finished fabric—her family. What a rewarding career—for in the end they rise up and praise her.

Here are some of her characteristics as a home manager: reflector of inner beauty as developed from walking with God, trustworthy partner, careful budgeter rather than a spendthrift, submissive wife, committed helpmeet, tender lover, cheerful homemaker, tidy housekeeper, interior decorator, purchasing agent, alert manager of her time, creative cook, chauffeur, businesswoman, wise investor of money, physical-fitness expert, maker of hand-stitchery, volunteer worker, compassionate neighbor, wardrobe planner, clothes designer, wife of a busy husband, creative seamstress, student of the Word, one who daily walks with the Lord—an example of a gracious and godly woman. Her husband has assigned her the management of the home—an area in which to make decisions and sharpen her wits. She certainly need not feel inferior or suppressed. In fact, at times she may feel that it is more than she can handle, or she may look upon it as the exciting challenge in life that she was seeking.

The success of the home manager depends upon her attitude of heart toward the job. There is much room for creative self-improvement in every area of the Proverbs woman's career. Or she can decide that this routine is drudgery and that "I am a prisoner in my own home." The Spirit-filled home manager will develop her capabilities and say in her heart, "Whatsoever you do, do it heartily as unto the Lord."

The Wife as Lover

The Bible does not say much to wives about loving their husbands, yet husbands are commanded several times to love their wives. The woman seems to have an emotional nature that makes it easier for her to love. The husband apparently possesses a one-track mind which can get involved in his business, sports, or other activities, and thus he needs to be reminded to love his wife. She can assist the husband in remembering that he is to love her by being as neat and attractive as possible. Love is not a one-sided affair. It develops out of mutual esteem and admiration for one another.

As that feeling grows, it can be expressed beautifully by the intimacy of the act of marriage. The wife need not be afraid to enjoy this relationship with her husband, for it was designed by God. The Creator saw that it was not good for Adam to be alone, so He created Eve and said that they were to become one flesh. Normally the woman is a "responder" to her husband's love, but it is in God's order for her to be the "initiator" from time to time. According to 1 Corinthians 7:3, 4: "Let the husband fulfill his duty to his wife, and likewise also the wife to her husband. The wife does not have authority over her own body, but the husband does; and likewise also the husband does not have authority over his body, but the wife does" (NAS). The next verse charges both spouses: "Stop depriving one another . . . ." Many of us grew up in an era which believed that nice ladies did not admit they enjoyed the act of

answer for herself before God, so I respect what God has led you to do, and hope that you respect God's leading in my life, too.

Discipline Your Body

What difference does outward adornment make? It matters much, because a woman's appearance, her grooming, and her size are indications of who controls her life—Jesus Christ or self. Ouch! That sounds harsh, but I am also talking about myself! The times I have let down on my appearance, or my weight has jumped, have been periods that have not been controlled by my Heavenly Father. It was during a time when a lack of self-discipline, or self-carelessness or self-pity took over. Accept yourself just as you are and then proceed to ask God to help you change the things that can be changed. After your next bath, take a good look at yourself in the mirror and commit every roll and bulge to Jesus Christ. Ask for wisdom and discipline into bringing those bulges under control. The same total discipline that causes us to study the Word and have a consistent prayer life will also help us in controlling our weight. I have known some people who had such severe "fat attacks" that they literally had to pray before eating any food. It was not a prayer of thanksgiving but a prayer which involved presenting one's body to Jesus Christ and asking for control of one's mouth and what was put into it.

Is there any difference between oversmoking, overdrinking, or overeating? The Bible condemns gluttony, drinking, and abuse of our bodies. I have a friend who cannot stop smoking. She has tried every device and plan and has failed in her attempts. I carry a great concern for her because she is a dear friend. She is on my prayer list, and I remember her often. That is all well and good, but on the other hand I have other dear friends who are victims of overstuffing and

I often fail to carry a burden to pray for them. Smoking and excessive eating are equally harmful to the body, and both are considered as sins. When a woman is Christ-controlled, she will have the desire to lead a disciplined life that will affect her outward appearance.

Let me leave a note in the minds of the ladies who are naturally trim and have no weight problem—beware of spiritual pride because you are not overweight. Be patient and pray for your not-so-thin sisters, remembering that you probably have other areas of weakness that they do not have.

Framing the Picture

Our outward adorning should not be extreme, nor should it call attention to our outer self. There are some who feel that all cosmetics are wrong; others do not wear any jewelry. Still others wear a good supply of cosmetics plus a variety of rings, earrings, and so on. What is right? "And let not your adornment be external only—braiding the hair, and wearing gold jewelry, and putting on dresses; but let it be the hidden person of the heart, with the imperishable quality of a gentle and quiet spirit, which is precious in the sight of God" (1 Peter 3:3, 4 NAS). This is not saying that *all* outward adorning is wrong. However, when it takes priority over the inner adornment, it is sinful. The examples of braiding the hair, wearing gold jewelry, and putting on dresses were all very typical practices of the Greeks and the Romans. Much time and effort was put on fancy hairstyles, and women entwined gold jewelry and fancy stones into their hair. The dresses of that day were made from costly silks and brocades. When all of these adornments were given higher priority than the attitude of the heart toward spiritual things, they were wrong.

It is obvious that putting on a dress is not wrong, nor is

fixing the hair or wearing jewelry; it all depends on what place these practices have in our lives. The verses in First Peter speak to us of cutting short some of the time we spend in outer embellishment, and putting it into studying the Word of God. The adornment should not be merely external. In other words, it is good to have some external help, but there should be more emphasis put on the hidden woman of the heart. All too often we are guilty of looking only at the outward adornment of others and forgetting the hidden person within. On the other hand, it is possible for the inner beauty to be difficult to see because of the rundown condition of the outer shell. It is highly possible for our outward appearance to resemble a potentially good dinner that is served helter-skelter. All the healthy, delicious ingredients are there to make an excellent meal, but they are just slopped on the plate without order or design. Why not have a proper balance? Let the outward appearance be as a frame to surround the picture of the hidden person of the heart. A beautifully framed picture is one that does not draw attention to the frame, but rather the frame aids the viewer to center the attention on the picture itself. And so it is with us. Our frame should not detract from the real person inside. Instead, it should contribute to focusing the attention on the real person—the hidden, inner woman.

I am reminded of the biblical Esther who was given one year for self-improvement. God wanted her to be beautiful to fulfill His purpose for her. She checked in at the "Shushan Physical Improvement Spa" and took all the beauty treatments they had to offer. The first six months she was treated with oil of myrrh, and then six months were given to skin care with spices and cosmetics. That is quite a difference from the ten minutes I spend each day, if I can squeeze it in. No wonder Esther won all the beauty contests of her day! But what a woman she was—obedient to God's

direction, patient to fit into His time schedule, and coura-
geous to fulfill a difficult role.

There seems to be a growing tendency across our country
for young people to have the "natural look." It can be very
attractive if done in good taste, but some such efforts have
gone beyond the natural and have resulted in an unflattering
unnatural look. The unkempt, faded, wrinkled look does
not represent the kind of godly person whom the Word uses
as an example. In fact, I firmly believe that this kind of
appearance is saying to the world that the Christ this person
serves is not able to fulfill the promise of Philippians 4:19:
"And my God shall supply all your needs according to His
riches in glory in Christ Jesus" (NAS). The Proverbs woman
is described as wearing beautiful clothes of purple and pure
linen, and yet she is described as a truly godly woman who
fears and reverences God. Her outward adornment did not
take priority over grooming the hidden person of the heart.

THE INNER BEAUTY

It is called "the hidden person of the heart" in 1 Peter
3:4. The Bible emphasizes that our priority should be in
developing this inner person. It is this quality of the gentle
and quiet spirit that is precious in the sight of God. This
does not mean that all spiritual women should act like Total
Phlegmatics. On the contrary! God created all of us as
unique individuals with varying combinations of the four
temperaments. So why would He tell us to be gentle and
quiet, when that is a natural characteristic of the Phlegmatic? A gentle and quiet spirit is one who has learned to be
tranquil and constant in the face of all circumstances. The
Choleric and Sanguine are both known to be noisy and
explosive. To have a gentle and quiet spirit comes only as a
result of working on our attitudes and walking in the Spirit.

"Thou wilt keep him in perfect peace, whose mind is stayed on thee . . ." (Isaiah 26:3).

Here we begin to distinguish where our priorities really are. Most of us have only a limited amount of time for which we can choose what we want to do. Very few women can join the bowling team, take tennis lessons, join a weekly ladies' Bible study, become members of the garden club, and participate in the weekly visitation program of the church—all at one time. So we have to pick and choose and sort out our priorities. It may come to the point where there is time for only one extra activity. What will it be? We can rationalize and say, "But I owe it to myself . . ." or "It will make me a more versatile woman . . ." but we must consider what effect it has on the hidden woman of the heart. Will it aid in developing a gentle and quiet spirit which is precious in the sight of God?

The beauty in a woman is seen when her life shows forth the fruit of the Spirit. That can only come from walking in fellowship with Jesus Christ: "But I say, walk by the Spirit, and you will not carry out the desire of the flesh" (Galatians 5:16 NAS). The woman who walks in the Spirit will portray the fruit of the Spirit—love, joy, peace, patience, kindness, goodness, faithfulness, gentleness, and self-control. Regardless of what her physical features may be like, she will have an inner glow and beauty that shines more brightly than her outward appearance. Her daily walk will be the key to the hidden woman of the heart. If she walks by fulfilling her own desires of the flesh, then her life will demonstrate that. But if she walks in the control of the Holy Spirit, she will live with the fruit of the Spirit in her life. That can only be done by studying the Word of God, fellowshiping with Him in prayer, and carrying a daily commitment to let God's will be accomplished in her life. It will change her attitudes, actions, and reactions. This kind of walk does not depend on how gracefully our feet and legs move. On the contrary! A lady can move with all the flowing smoothness of a Paris model and still have a "daily walk" that represents a mangled, crippled inner person. I have known godly women who had a beautiful walk in their daily inner lives, but whose body movements were clumsy and faltering. Inner beauty does not depend on a graceful body, but on our intimate, consistent relationship with Jesus Christ.

The Wife as a Mother-Teacher

One young mother told me that she felt as if she were running a seven-day-a-week, twenty-four-hour-a-day preschool or baby-sitting service. When a mother is right in the middle of this period, it seems as if it will never end, and her efforts can show no immediate results. If she could only stand back and take a look at the overall picture, it would encourage her heart and she could be more diligent in her efforts. Unfortunately, most mothers cannot do that—so I would like to help them see the picture through my eyes.

Children need mothers for more than receiving life. That is only the small beginning. When that unique little creation arrives on the scene, there is an aura of mystery surrounding him. He has all the features of an adult but in such miniature form. A baby enters the world with much fanfare and expectancy, and yet does nothing to return this love to the very woman who gave birth to him. He is totally dependent on outside help and has nothing to give in return. What a challenge and dedication on the part of the mother! The child needs the tender care of a mother who will serve him unselfishly and untiringly without expecting much in return for the first few months of life.

"Children are a gift from God; they are his reward"

(Psalms 127:3 LB). I can just hear some of you young mothers sigh with disagreement, because there are certain times when they appear more like a punishment than a reward. After spending the night walking the floor with a screaming child, or hearing the school principal tell you that your child is failing in all of his subjects, or finding out that your child is heavily into drugs, it is not too hard to understand why some parents feel that their child is a punishment rather than a reward. Yet children are a gift from God, and with the gift He has sent a book of instructions on how to train and prepare that gift for life.

The Complete Instruction Book

One year we gave our sons a Christmas gift of a detailed Erector Set. With that set came a complete book of instructions, and our boys were able to enjoy the gift because they followed the instructions. Without that help, the gift would have been worthless and a real frustration. Beautiful, complex designs were built because they read the manual carefully and followed what it said. The manufacturer knew what potential the Erector Set held, so he published the instruction book for the benefit and enjoyment of the gift's receiver. The Creator of all children has sent along an instruction book so that His gift might be enjoyed. When the instructions are followed, one can expect to develop the potential and capabilities of a child into a beautiful complex design with real purpose and reward. Our two sons would read the instructions for the Erector Set and sometimes disagree on how a design should be done. It was important for them to agree on how to do it, in order to accomplish the more complex constructions. Likewise, moms and dads need to agree and be united on the "how to" before they can expect many results. The Book of Proverbs gives more instruction on raising and training children than any other single book in the Bible. A chapter of this book should be read by parents every day—and it should be read over and over again.

It is difficult to separate the roles of mother and teacher because so much of the mother's job description turns out to be a teaching responsibility. Ephesians 6 tells the father to be the overseer of the discipline and instruction of the children. But the mother, as the helpmeet, must share in this project and carry out the standards that have been agreed upon. The mother spends more waking hours with the child than the father, so it is essential that they work together as a team.

Parents United

Probably some of our most heartbreaking counseling sessions have been when mothers and fathers have failed to be united on the teaching and disciplining of their children. When the years begin to reveal that their divided spirits have produced havoc and despair, they come to us with troubled hearts about their rebellious children. Young parents would avoid some of these traumatic problems if they would agree to be united in disciplining their children at an early age. Children catch on very young when Mom and Dad do not agree, and they begin to play one parent against the other. How much more effective rules and regulations would be if both parents would stand firmly united together.

A simple formula which I proposed in *How to Develop Your Child's Temperament* can be put to good use by all mothers:

Instruction + Love + Insistence = Effective Training

It requires all three of these ingredients to have effective training. If any two are used without the third, the training will be inadequate.

The joy of training comes when you begin to see results happening. It may take months and years, but be diligent and "not weary in well doing," because the day will come when you can put away your role of teacher and enjoy the rewards of the gift. If you give up too early, you will live under the regret that you should have stuck with it—and your children would have been different. None of us is perfect. We look back over the last twenty-nine years of parenthood and realize we have made a lot of mistakes. But somehow we had the direction from our Heavenly Father that our children would be reluctant in obeying Jesus Christ if they did not first learn to obey their parents. We are thankful today that this strong principle of obedience covers over many of the mistakes we made. Our four children are all walking with the Lord and are sensitive to His leading. It is not because they had such good examples from their mother and father, but because they were raised on biblical principles right out of the "complete instruction book."

6

The Roles of the Husband

It is not easy to be a good husband. But it is difficult to be good at anything—from marriage to sports to scholarship. If you're going to do something, you might just as well become as proficient as you can. Fortunately, we Christians are not like the secular sophisticates of our time, who reject all basic guidelines to life and maintain that each generation must find for itself the best way to live. If the automotive industry operated that way, we would still be immersed in the Model T stage. Doubtless that is the reason for so much unhappiness in the average family—its members are always stumbling around, trying to find the right way to operate.

The Spirit-controlled family is attentive to God's manual on human behavior, the Bible, which gives explicit instructions as to how the family should function. The next diagram shows the variety of roles God planned for the husband. His contribution to family happiness will be determined by how well he assumes each of these roles.

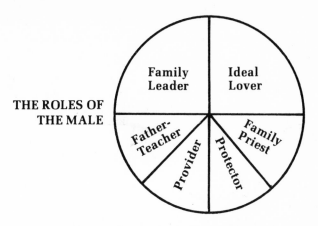

THE ROLES OF
THE MALE

Family
Leader

Ideal
Lover

Father-
Teacher

Provider

Protector

Family
Priest

The Husband as Family Leader

God's first assignment for the husband is to be the leader of his family. Our text in Ephesians 5:23 clearly states, "For the husband is the head of the wife, even as Christ is the head of the church: and he is the saviour of the body." This accords with Genesis 3:16, where God says to the woman: ". . . and thy desire shall be to thy husband, and he shall rule over you." This principle is repeated in 1 Corinthians 11:3: "But I would have you know, that the head of every man is Christ; and the head of the woman is the man . . . ."

Before any young man takes a bride from the protective custody of her father's home, he had better be ready to assume her leadership. It matters not that she is a quick-acting Choleric and he a passive Phlegmatic—she needs a leader. The most frustrated women today are those who interpret advice of the Women's Lib movement as a call to dominate their husbands. In the "book of beginnings" (Genesis), where God laid out the tracks of life for people to run on, He said that a woman's desire shall be to her husband. That is, her basic psychic mechanism is to be a follower to that man who opens his life, home, and possessions to her. Once she marries such a man, her natural inclination is to follow him. If he shirks the role of leadership out of neglect, ignorance (because he did not see such a role exemplified by his father or does not know the Bible), or personal weakness, he is damning his wife to a lifetime of psychic frustration. Such women gradually become carnal, dominating, neurotic, and obnoxious as the years roll by. It is very difficult for a woman to submit to a man who refuses to lead. A young man best serves God, his wife, and himself when he starts immediately to assume the role of leader in his home. There are plenty of opportunities for the strong-willed wife to use her Choleric tendencies, but being the leader of her home is not one of them!

Respect is not innate, as is love. It must be earned, and all husbands should remember that. If your children do not respect you as the head of the home, your entire family is in trouble. I have seen children who loved their father, but felt sorry for him because he was not exercising leadership in their home. One such daughter at twenty-four, a physical-education instructor in the public schools and a tennis star, could not relate to her husband, for she was bound up with hate and bitterness toward her mother. Finally the story came out. Her dad was a generous, kindly baker who receded into a shell and succumbed to his wife's intense domination. Clenching her teeth, the daughter growled, "My greatest desire in high school was that just once my daddy would double up his fist and belt my mother in the mouth." Anything short of male leadership in the home has a disastrous effect on each member of the family.

Whenever we speak of male leadership in the home, we tend to equate it with the old European paternalistic family where father was a virtual dictator. Such a role, though still common in many homes in northeastern Europe, does not coincide with biblical teaching. God's leadership standard is *always* set before us in love, as we shall see later in this chapter. The husband is to serve as leader of the wife—*as Christ is the head of the church.* That constitutes a leadership of love. Our Lord directs us, leads us, makes decisions for us, and takes responsibility for us in a spirit of love and consideration, always maintaining a supreme interest in our good.

The difference between male leadership in the home and *loving* male leadership is that when the husband is forced to make a decision that counters the desires of his wife and children, he must exercise his prerogative in love. "How can the family be assured of that?" you may ask. Very simple. In whose best interest is the decision being made? The husband's? Selfishness has no place in the Spirit-filled home. A loving leader will always make his final decision for the good of the family. Since he is human, he may not always be right, but his motivation should always be directed toward the good of all.

The husband's role of leadership is much like that of the president of a corporation. Many employees work under him, some of whom, like his wife, are his equals, and some his superiors, at least intellectually. Andrew Carnegie used to boast that his success could not be attributed to his skills alone, but to the fact that he hired subordinates who were more capable than he. Would such an administrator dictate over superior people? Never. To gain their greatest productivity, he will allow them as much freedom as possible within the corporate structure, always considering their thoughts and opinions when making decisions. Similarly, a wise husband will consider the feelings and ideas of the wife and the children (as the latter mature). Many times he will concur with their arguments, but that does not in one degree lessen his leadership. On occasion, however, he may reject their input and render an unpopular verdict. I would offer five considerations in such a case:

1. Never make a decision without hearing and evaluating the wife's views.
2. Always pray for the decision-making wisdom which God promises to provide (James 1:5).
3. Always check your motivation. Is it really for the family's good, or could it be inspired by selfishness or prejudice?
4. Use tact in effecting your decision—a sensitive father will not alienate the family he loves.
5. Once the decision is made, do not give in under pressure (pouting, temper, frigidity, or any other manifestations of carnality). However, always be open to further evidence that might render your decision obsolete and warrant a change. In the plan of God, the husband should make the final decisions.

Leadership is not an easy role to maintain, and at times, during the aftermath of a decision, the leader can get mighty lonely. To be honest, I don't always like making family decisions, but that's part of my job—and husbands, it's yours too. God holds you accountable as the corporate head of your home. Be fair, be reasonable, be loving—but by all means, be a leader.

Decision making becomes more complex as the family grows. As seen in the next diagram, the mother who functions as a manager—working more closely with the children and the home than does the father—is apt to make decisions primarily from that perspective. The father has to evaluate her suggestions, but from a broader perspective. It is a wise wife who tries to understand her husband's decision if they can't afford a vacation, new clothes for the children, or a new item of furniture. He may be thinking ahead about a

GOD'S LINES OF AUTHORITY

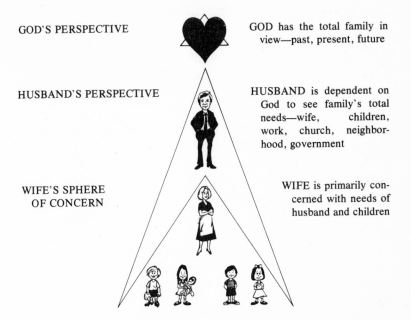

GOD'S PERSPECTIVE   GOD has the total family in view—past, present, future

HUSBAND'S PERSPECTIVE   HUSBAND is dependent on God to see family's total needs—wife, children, work, church, neighborhood, government

WIFE'S SPHERE OF CONCERN   WIFE is primarily concerned with needs of husband and children

possible layoff, taxes, or house repairs. One of the most difficult areas of interpersonal relationships arises when we attempt to see life through the eyes of another person. Ideally, in spite of temperament differences, couples should see things alike as their love matures.

NOTE TO HUSBANDS—THE OTHER SIDE OF SUBMISSION

Before passing from this subject, two brief notes to husbands are in order. The first concerns submission from the woman's perspective. It is not easy for a strong-willed woman to submit to a man "in everything." Even a Spirit-filled Choleric wife will have to learn that role. You can help as a husband by being fair in carefully attending to her point of view and even accepting it whenever possible without relinquishing your role as leader. If you are predominantly Melancholy and your wife Choleric, don't be surprised if many of her suggestions are more practical than yours. The wise husband is man enough to admit that quite often her ideas are better than his.

In our case, Bev usually takes longer to make a decision than I, but if she makes up her mind in time, her judgment is often best. I learned years ago that she will not be pressured into quick decisions. In fact, she will invariably throw ice water on anything suddenly thrust upon her. In our early, selfish days, that became a bone of contention, for when I evaluated a proposal and pressed my decision upon her, she would balk—but I would force her to go along with me. Oh, she didn't scream and holler—Phlegmatics don't do that—but she was superb at clamming up and dragging her feet. I thoroughly enjoyed my role as "enforcer," but my gestapo tactics did nothing for our marriage. Now I have learned to spring nothing on her quickly. Instead, in love, I plan long-range and give her plenty of lead time. In fact, a good approach is: "Honey, I've got an idea; don't give me a decision now, but think it over." Then I share the plan and back off for a few days. About 85 percent of the time she agrees with me or improves my idea by the time we discuss it again. The other 15 percent of the time we either abandon the idea or she goes along joyfully, now that she too is filled with the Spirit.

The point is to go out of your way to adapt your leadership to the temperament and personhood needs of your wife. Her agreement and submission do not have to come at the expense of her self-respect—if you will let her express herself and then demonstrate that you value her opinion. For instance, never forget that she is a far greater authority on the needs of your children than you are. She has spent ten times as many hours with them by their fifth birthday than you have and consequently knows them better. I wish every husband could sit in the counseling room and hear a well-educated, intelligent, and loving wife exclaim, "The most maddening thing about my husband is his refusal to listen to my side of the argument." Wives don't want agreement as much as they want a platform to air their views. We could all learn from the results of an international survey taken by the League of Large Families in Brussels (cited in *The Seven Stumbling Blocks Ahead of Husbands*, a publication of The American Institute of Family Relations), indicating the seven most common failings of husbands, in the opinions of wives:

1. A lack of tenderness
2. A lack of politeness
3. A lack of sociability
4. A failure to understand the wife's temperament and peculiarities
5. Unfairness in financial matters
6. Frequency of snide remarks and sneers at the wife before company or the children
7. A lack of plain honesty and truthfulness

Handling Spirit-Filled Disagreements

Even two people filled with the Spirit will not experience total agreement on everything. If that were a requirement, Bev and I would be disqualified, for we see everything differently. I like to work furiously right up to departure time for a vacation, pack the car, then as I'm backing out of the driveway prior to a three-thousand-mile trip ask, "Would you look in the glove compartment and see if you can find a map?" Bev is the type who contacts the automobile club two months in advance to plan a basic strategy for the trip. That difference shows itself in all our decisions—from breakfast cereal to wallpaper. We are more surprised when we agree than when we disagree.

Soon after being filled with the Spirit, we developed a very simple procedure that has helped resolve those contrary choices. Whenever it is "comfortable" to do so, one of us agrees with the other (about 40 percent of the time each of us "gives in" about 20 percent). The remaining 60 percent of our disagreements are settled by agreeing to "pray about it." God has promised to give His children wisdom when they ask, and we have found that He really does. He will cause one of us to acquiesce joyfully with the other's point of view, or many times He will lead us to an entirely different decision. The number of times I am forced to make a final decision which is unpleasant to Bev thus becomes infrequent.

Being a Good Leader

The second note on submission from a woman's viewpoint is that it is easier for her to respect a man who will stand up and be a good leader. All temperaments possess a natural weakness in leadership which must be strengthened. Cholerics are strong, aggressive leaders who need to develop compassion and consideration of others. Sanguines are prone to be inconsistent leaders, quick to make impossible decisions which they expect the wife to execute. They need to make fewer but more deliberate decisions and implement them graciously. Melancholies tend to be legalistic nit-pickers who would return with the family toward Old Testament or pharisaical rules and even then find something to criticize. They need to be leaders known for their "sweet reasonableness." The Phlegmatic needs to work on being a more aggressive leader. He prefers to head for a garage after work and putter around his workbench, abdicating his leadership role to the wife at a time when his teenagers are making life-molding decisions and evaluations.

A missionary wife came to us in tears after our seminar in their base city in Asia, saying, "I am losing all respect for my husband. He leaves all the discipline of our three teen-age children to me." This man, interestingly enough, was a very effective missionary. But strong home leadership was difficult for him, so rather than trust the Holy Spirit for the self-control and goodness He promises, he was reaping a lifetime of relinquished leadership at a desperate period in his teenagers' lives. A case in point she shared was his treatment of their TV viewing, one of the biggest bones of contention in most Christian homes, if the problem is not solved before the children reach five years of age. As the moral standards of TV entertainment ("corruption" is a better word) were plunging to all-time lows, he took strong exception to the immoral programs his children watched, but left the execution of his standards to his wife. If he came home and found them watching something he disapproved of, he would run to her and complain, "You're letting those children watch one of those programs I have forbidden." When she responded, "Well, you tell them to shut it off," he would reply, "That's your job." Thus the spiritual head of the family abrogated his role and played second-string to his wife, even though God has given men a deeper register of voice and a masculine, commanding bearing that makes discipline of the older children much easier for them than for the wives. I found under similar circumstances that the situation merely required me to affect the lowest commanding voice I could muster and say, "Kids, do you want to turn that program off or do you want me to?" That was the signal which opened two options: (1) They turned the channel to a more acceptable program; or (2) I turned the TV off altogether.

Love and respect run on the same street: one will not endure long without the other. To keep her love you must earn her respect, and believe me, you need her respect!

The Husband as Ideal Lover

After God, the greatest love in a man's life should be his wife. He is commanded to love her more than he loves his neighbor, for Ephesians 5:25 states he is to love her as Christ loved the church. He is told only to love his neighbor "as himself." The Greek work for *love* here is the same used in John 3:16 and other passages to describe God's love for man in sacrificing His Son. For that reason we say a man should love his wife sacrificially.

The late Dr. Harry Ironside, my favorite Bible teacher, once told of a young husband who came to him wondering if he loved his wife so much that it interfered with his love for the Lord. The lad said she was the center of his first thought in the morning, the last at night. He would call her several times a day. Even when he prayed, he couldn't get her out of his mind. Wise old Dr. Ironside asked, "Young man, do you love her enough to die for her?" After hesitating for a moment, he replied, "No, I guess not," to which the aged counselor responded, "Your problem is, you don't love her enough!"

No emotion is more needed, more talked about, and less understood than love. Poems by the reams have been written about it; stories, plays, and movies have portrayed it; mankind never tires of hearing about it—yet except for mother love the reality of its expression is seldom experienced. True husband love is supernatural, a result of being filled with the fruit of the Spirit. That kind of love is a treasure that grows and matures through the years, not depending on any single event but requiring a lifetime to express. As the result of a man and woman sharing their total selves unconditionally, it can absorb conflict, disagreement, disappointment, tragedy, and even selfishness. It is not dependent on two perfect persons, but on two people filled with the Spirit of God. Love is the ideal way to face the unknown and potentially bumpy road to the future. It is to marriage what shock absorbers are to a car—it cushions the rough spots in life. A husband who nurtures a love like that is guaranteed a steady return on his investment (Galatians 6:7, 8). It is well worth a lifetime of cultivation.

TEST YOUR LOVE

Through the years we have been asked to develop a test that would basically reveal a husband's love for his wife. The following questions are quite revealing. You may score yourself 0–10 on each of them. Read them carefully and try to be objective.

1. ____ Do you have a strong and affectionate bond of caring about your wife's needs and desires that inspires a willingness on your part to sacrifice to fulfill them?
2. ____ Do you enjoy her personality, companionship, and friendship?
3. ____ Do you share common goals and interests which you communicate about freely?
4. ____ Do you respect and admire her in spite of recognized needs or weaknesses in her life?
5. ____ Do you have sexual attraction for each other that leads frequently to a mutually satisfactory expression of the act of marriage?
6. ____ Do you desire children (if physically possible) who share both of your physical and temperament characteristics and to whom you can impart your moral and spiritual values?

7. ____ Do you have a vital faith in God that is a helpful influence on her spiritual life?
8. ____ Do you have a sense of permanence and possession about her such that other women are not in like manner attractive to you?
9. ____ Do you have a growing desire to be with her?
10. ____ Do you have a genuine appreciation for your wife's successes?

____ TOTAL SCORE

If you scored 90 to 100, you are doing well. If in the 80s, you need to work on your love. A score in the 70s suggests that your deficiencies are getting serious, and below 70 indicates that you need help soon! You must not only "walk in the Spirit," but you should consult your pastor.

WHAT IS LOVE?

Everyone agrees that love is a feeling. Where it comes from or how one gets it inspires a variety of answers. As a feeling, love is a motivator that causes action, and for that reason the best way to define love is to examine what it does. The diagram on the next page, based on 1 Corinthians 13:4–8, particularly applies to a husband's love for his wife, for it describes the way he will treat her when he is controlled by the Holy Spirit. In fact, inadequacy in any of these nine expressions of love is a sure indication that he is more filled with himself and his own spirit than the sacrificial love imparted by the Holy Spirit.

1 CORINTHIANS 13: 4-8.

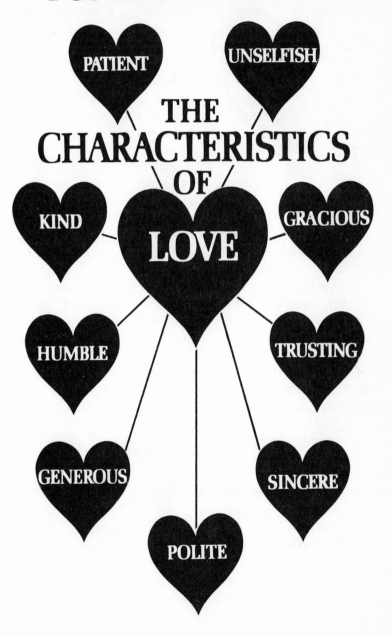

THE CHARACTERISTICS OF LOVE

PATIENT

UNSELFISH

KIND

LOVE

GRACIOUS

HUMBLE

TRUSTING

GENEROUS

SINCERE

POLITE

True love is patient or enduring, as the Greek word really indicates. Most translators label this word "long-suffering." That is, it will accept slights and rebuffs lovingly or without retaliation. A good test of this is how you respond during your wife's menstrual period. She needs extra love and tender warmth at a time when she may be less lovable. It is a wise husband who anticipates that time of the month—or any other of his wife's pressure points—and goes out of his way to show his love regardless of her attitude.

One husband said, "I love my wife, but I get so impatient with her sometimes. What's wrong?" I answered, "Your problem is that you love yourself at those impatient times more than you love your wife. Otherwise you would be patient."

Henry Drummond said years ago, "Love understands and therefore waits." Bill Gothard today observes, "Lust cannot wait to get; love cannot wait to give."

To a woman, the king of all expressions of love is kindness. Women are stronger emotionally than we think. A woman can suffer hurt, offense, and pain far better than a man, but in the home she is particularly vulnerable to unkindness from her husband or children. That is especially

true of words. Most men do not realize that just as they are visually stimulated, the wife is verbally responsive. The man who comes home from work and barks out criticism, demands, and insults is not only exhibiting carnality but is committing sexual suicide. The lover who walks in at night filled with *love, joy,* and *peace* will resort to kind words and tender speech. He is motivated purely by love and respect for his wife, but is in fact preparing them both to culminate their many expressions of love in the act of marriage sometime during the evening. Love is its own reward.

Love expresses itself in many kind ways—gifts, flowers, unexpected remembrances, and a host of thoughtful gestures that are meaningful to a wife. All wives do not have the same temperament, so what turns one woman on may be meaningless to another. Find out what your wife likes and responds to—then express your love tangibly. My wife, for example, prefers flowers. Personally, I think they are a waste! If I had my way, we would install plastic flowers in our home, for they require no watering, pruning, or care, yet they would always look nice. There is just one thing wrong with that idea—Bev hates plastic flowers. Consequently, I still buy flowers from the kid on the corner, just to lighten her day. During the five years I shared with other speakers at seminars, I would always stop on Saturday nights at the flower counter at the San Diego Airport and bring home a bouquet of yellow roses. They did nothing for me, but they sure turned Bev on—and that's what counts. I know—you're running out of ideas for gifts. So am I! After thirty-one birthdays, Christmases, anniversaries, Valentine's Days, "sweetest days," and other miscellaneous events, my creativity has been shredded. But kindness keeps us faithful, and it's the thought that counts.

When I put the hand of our daughter Linda into the hand of "Murph" and "gave her away," I had an opportunity that only we preacher fathers enjoy—I also performed the wedding ceremony. Looking into that young man's eyes, I was rather startled at how young he looked. The full reality of the moment gripped me. I was entrusting the first treasure of our home, the product of twenty years of love, into his inexperienced hand. (Naturally I forgot that Bev's dad had done the same to me years before.) Speaking for fathers everywhere, I said to my new son, "Murph, Linda's mom and I don't ask that you make her rich or famous, but we do make one special request as you take her from our home— always be kind to her." I thank God that he has honored that charge faithfully, as her love for him has demonstrated.

True love is so generous that it takes genuine delight in the successes of one's partner. A man in our church can't so much as sing in the shower, but his wife has a beautiful voice. I like to watch him when she sings, for the expression on his face testifies that no one in the church gets more enjoyment from her gift than he does. Contrast that to the man who is so immature that he has forbidden his wife to sing in the choir because he would rather have her sit with him in church. She is being submissive, of course, but not to a loving and sensitive husband. Generous love will spill over into the way a couple spends money, entertains, invests in charitable projects, or in other ways utilizes their resources. Love is giving! The best way to get love is to give it away.

Pride is the greatest single enemy which man faces in life. In 1 Peter 5 and James 4 .Satan is pictured as a roaring lion, seeking to devour man through pride. A proud spirit is a destroyer of true love and therefore has no place in the life of a Spirit-controlled husband, whose love inspires him to forget himself and his "rights" in deference to the emotional and material needs of the family. I am never impressed with the husband whose garage is filled with the latest power tools, or whose closet bursts with the best sporting gear, but whose wife is still limited in the kitchen to wedding-gift equipment or hand-me-down utensils.

Electronic door openers and other mechanical contrivances, together with the self-sufficiency tone of our times, do nothing to cultivate courtesy and polite behavior. I have been appalled throughout my travels around the world to see how men have neglected good manners. Many a man no longer opens doors for his wife or remembers which side of the sidewalk to escort her on. Women, of course, are quite capable of opening doors for themselves, but men need to cultivate these gestures of respect. Women of all ages enjoy being treated as someone "special."

I have probably opened 25,000 doors for the special women in my life (Bev and the three girls), and I anticipate another 25,000 before the friendly undertaker lays me to rest. I not only enjoy treating them like ladies, but I am gratified by the sense of self-worth such actions engender in a woman. One of our daughters dated a Christian young man whom we didn't fully approve of. He met all of our basic conditions for dating, but there was something crude about him that just didn't inspire me. One date was all it took for our teenager to come home and announce, "Ugh! That's the last time I'm going out with that clod! He doesn't even know how to treat a girl." A few years later, when she wrote to tell us about the lad she met in a Christian college, she attached the following P.S.: "Dad, you'll like him; he treats me like a real lady."

If Jesus Christ, the embodiment of love, were here on earth today, He would treat all women as ladies. We husbands can hardly do less for those lovely creatures who bear our names.

We have already observed how selfishness is a matrimonial destroyer. Love, we hasten to add, will erase selfishness and self-seeking, and Spirit-controlled love will look for ways to express itself. Every couple has different tastes that usually do not reveal themselves until after marriage. I am a sports nut, my wife a lover of culture. To her credit Bev has, in love, cultivated a genuine interest in athletics. We hold season tickets to the San Diego Charger games and occasionally attend basketball, baseball, and hockey events. Although I love her dearly, I cannot honestly share her enthusiasm for opera or the symphony. Oh, I take her on occasion (even though it leaves me a little numb), but very truthfully my basic enjoyment that evening comes from viewing the obvious pleasure it instills in her. You should have seen her the night I took her to hear the Boston Philharmonic Symphony Orchestra play Tchaikovsky's Fifth Symphony in E minor. I won't tell you how I felt (it wasn't a total loss, however; I designed a chart on the Book of Revelation with special emphasis on the tribulation period)—but she loved it!

The best-tempered homes, as we have already seen, will be Spirit-controlled homes. The usual disharmony, short temper, and irritability will be replaced by the gracious love and peace of the Holy Spirit. Such love is not touchy, easily offended, or defensive, and it never responds in anger or hostility, either verbally or emotionally.

Jealousy is a cruel taskmaster and an unnecessary bedfellow in a Spirit-controlled marriage. Usually it is generated by the insecurities of one partner more than by the deeds of the other. Many couples return from parties or group activities in the midst of violent quarrels because the flirtations or provocations of one have fanned the

jealousies of the other. True love is trusting and "thinketh
no evil." Solomon warns against "evil surmisings." If you
have a temperament that is easily given to such thoughts,
always evaluate the situation through the magnifying glass
of love. A loving spirit not only goes the extra mile but is
quick to excuse. Self-love is quick to condemn.

Deceit is harmful to any relationship between people, but
it is devastating in a marriage.
Some of the most heartrend-
ing cases I know have in-
volved women who said, "I
cannot trust my husband."
The tragedy of deceit lies in
its principal quality—it never
remains static. The man who
tells his wife "little white
lies" soon starts to feed her
"gray" and ultimately "big black" lies. Some wives cannot
trust their husbands in any area—financially, morally, and
so on. I can verify that the immoral man cannot be trusted
in anything. Sexual sins lead to lying, financial manipula-
tions, and widespread deceit. Finally the culprit weaves
such a web for himself that he is caught in it and exposed.

True love not only is sincere but goes out of its way to be
honest—in word and deed. This is never more apparent
than after an argument. When the husband gradually comes
to the painful conclusion that he was either wrong or
reacted improperly, and that he owes his wife an apology,
what should he do? I have never found it easy to admit that
I acted unreasonably or made an erroneous decision. The
male ego seems to assert itself at that moment and declare,
"Serves her right! That one will make up for all the times

how to help them.) Several years ago I developed the following three steps which will ignite the most sputtering love.

1: Walk in the Spirit. Marriage is not a two-way relationship flowing between man and woman, It is a three-way relationship. As we walk in the Spirit, God gives us a love for each other which will flow spontaneously! A breakdown in our relationship as partners will inevitably entail a breakdown in our relationship with God. In fact, Bev and I have used a collapse between us as a signal that we were not walking in the Spirit. By confessing that sin to God, we opened our eyes to the problem.

2. Never dwell on insults, injuries, hurts, or the weaknesses of your partner.   Every person I have counseled for "lack of love" has developed a well-rehearsed list of grievances he can quickly impose upon his partner. This noxious response is similar to taking the lid off a septic tank, with all the poisons and stench of the past foaming out. If that sounds extreme to you, it is only because you have not heard the vile things people can think up about their partners. The Bible says, "As a man thinketh in his heart, so is he" (*see* Proverbs 23:7). The mouth becomes the potent revealer of thoughts. Evil, negative thoughts (even when true) are destructive of good feelings, and thus the Spirit-controlled Christian will not permit them to clutter his mind and clog his feelings.

3. Thank God for ten things about your partner, twice daily for three weeks. We have already noted that the Spirit-controlled Christian will consistently fulfill the mandate: "In everything give thanks." Constant griping corrupts good emotions, whereas thanksgiving cultivates them. I defy any man to make a list of ten qualities he likes about his wife, thank God each morning and every evening for them—and still have trouble loving her. (I also defy any man to gripe continually about his wife in his mind—and still maintain love for her.) The battle for love is won or lost in the mind, not the heart. Quite clearly, the heart is the servant of what the mind thinks.

The best illustration of this technique occurred several years ago when a friend confessed, "I don't love my wife anymore. In fact, we haven't slept in the same bedroom for three months." Together we scratched out, on a three-by-five card, ten things about her that he liked. He promised to review his list thankfully each morning during his quiet time and each evening during his thirty-five minute ride home from work. In ten days he enthusiastically exclaimed, "We're back in the same bedroom!" In three weeks he added, "I love that woman more now than in all the years of our marriage." When I asked him if he had memorized his list, he smiled and replied, "Oh, sure, I had that list learned the third day, so I turned the card over and wrote down fifteen more things I like about her."

No man can daily thank God for ten things about his wife without propagating love. You can imagine what love would be engendered if he raised his list to twenty-five. Several years have passed, and my friend and his wife have grown much closer for the most part, but a few months ago he sadly commented at lunch, "We're not sleeping together again!" I asked if he had lost his thanksgiving list, to which he replied, "I knew you were going to ask that!" Together we made another list—in spite of his reluctance to "try that again"—but it worked in just two weeks. Praise and thanksgiving are powerful factors for igniting love.

HUSBAND: WHY YOU?

Husbands may well ask, "Why does God command me four times to love my wife and only once direct her to love me?" That is a question I have pondered for many years and can offer two possible answers. First, women have a greater need to be loved. As one woman said, "Without love I have no life!" Second, men have a harder time loving. Because of their nature, women possess an enormous capacity for love, whereas men have to cultivate theirs. That is why a man should be very careful about walking in the control of the Spirit. He needs the supernatural love of God to be the lifetime lover God commands him to be, and that his wife naively expected him to be when she agreed to become his wife.

As a student of family living for many years, I have come to the conclusion that the man sets the love tone for his home. Women are basically responders to the treatment they are given. So far I have never seen a woman leave a man who is good to her, nor have I been asked to counsel a man who consistently cared for his wife. His expressions of love need not be costly, but they do need to represent that love honestly. While still a very young minister, one Friday night I was called into a wealthy home where the people had everything money could buy but shared no love. The next morning I visited the poorest family in our church to pray for their son who was about to leave for the army. Their home was so sparsely furnished that they had me sit at the end of their breakfast table on the edge of an orange crate. As we prayed, I was impressed with the love in this family, beginning with the father, whose wages were so low that their subsistence level was only ameliorated by an abundance of love!

LOVE AND HOUSEHOLD CHORES

In the old days on the farm there seemed to be a clear-cut separation between "his" duties and "hers." The wife was responsible for everything that went on inside the house, the man for everything outside. It is a wise and loving husband who has long since forgotten that outmoded idea. Now that the 140 acres outside have shrunk to a garage and a small yard, there is plenty of time to help the wife with the after-dinner dishes, take care of the children, and even change the baby's diapers (provided it is not harmful to the baby's health). If his wife has to work outside the home, the husband's in-house chore responsibilities will increase. When the wife is expecting—or after the baby arrives—it is again a tribute to his love when he willingly assumes some of those chores usually borne by the wife.

One word of caution is in order to the husband who wishes to show his love by helping around the house. Some wives, particularly in their youth, might interpret such willingness to help as an indication that the husband disapproves of their homemaking. Avoid this implication at all cost! Additionally, keep in mind that she is the manager of the house, so don't attempt to overhaul her system of doing things as though you were in charge of the household chores. In responsibility this is her domain. If in love you wish to volunteer to supplement efforts around the house, then subordinate yourself to her plan and household procedure. You have not abdicated your responsibility as head of the home to help fulfill your wife's plans at home. Management experts agree that one requirement of a good manager is that he first be a good follower. If your wife prefers to keep the everyday dishes high in the top cupboard where you have to stretch to get them, put them there. She doesn't tell you how to arrange your tools. You may in love try to suggest a more practical location, but be sure to take your tact pills before you do. Your thoughtful efforts to "help out" will usually be cheerfully accepted as long as you are willing to respect her household policies. Otherwise your good deed can become a bone of contention.

MAKE TIME FOR LOVE

The pressurized age in which we live seriously infringes upon our free time. In spite of our push-button appliances and timesaving electronic gadgetry, we have no more spare time available to us than did our forefathers. Personally, I think we do more things than they did, but I'm not sure we get more accomplished. I read somewhere that in 1900 the average man traveled a little over 1,000 miles annually; today almost all adult men average over 30,000 miles yearly. If that is true, they travel more every two years than Grandfather did in his lifetime. However, don't get in such a hurry that you have no time for love.

Many wives share a pet peeve: "My husband holds down two jobs [or one job and thirteen hobbies] and has no time for me." I often find their claim justified. Without realizing it, his merry-go-round of activities has become more crowded and speeded up until he can't stop it. A wise husband schedules into his activity book periodic "mini-honeymoons," occasional "dinners out," or some "couple time." That is particularly true after the children arrive. Tailor your outings to your budget, of course, but by all means have them. There is something exciting about a night in a motel without routine household attractions. It not only gives the couple a few hours to get reacquainted as persons, but it puts a mystery and spark into your love life. We recommend it at least once a quarter—oftener if you can afford it. To the wife it says, "I love you and I enjoy spending time with you."

VERBALIZE YOUR LOVE

Wherever I have the opportunity to share one important word of wisdom to husbands, it is: "Be careful to verbalize your love to your wife." A man often thinks that because he has little need for verbal reassurance of his wife's love, she is equally self-sufficient. Don't you believe it! Have you noticed how often a little girl will sit on her father's lap and ask, "Daddy, do you love me? Why don't you tell me?" In spite of their better-developed bodies and expensive hairdos, women are only girls grown tall, and they still thrive on hearing you verbalize your love. The more romantically you do it, the better.

I'm not altogether sure why women have this need to hear their husbands say repeatedly, "I love you. I love you. I love you," but they do, so you might as well get used to it. Perhaps they are the ones who took the greatest risk in this relationship, putting their absolute trust and confidence in us at such an early age that they were probably the only ones who dreamed we would ever amount to anything. They did it because they loved us and wanted us to love them in return. They need to be reassured regularly that we are keeping our part of the bargain.

As the parent of a married daughter, I can appreciate the beautiful story of the father who gave his daughter's husband-to-be a new watch as a wedding gift. When the lad popped up the gold cover the first time, he saw these words written across the face: SAY SOMETHING NICE TO SALLY

EACH DAY. Such a daily verbalization of your love will do much for your marriage.

In spite of his questionable character, I like Merlin's advice to King Arthur regarding his treatment of Lady Guinevere when she became his queen. He simply insisted, "Love her! Love her! Love her!" God said it even better: "Love her as Christ loved the church."

The Husband as Family Provider

From the very beginning, man was given the responsibility of being the family breadwinner. God said to Adam, "In the sweat of thy face shalt thou eat bread . . ." (Genesis 3:19). From that day on, the man has been accountable for both the financial provision and the psychological and physical protection of his family. In the New Testament, men are taught: "But if any provide not . . . for those of his own house, he hath denied the faith, and is worse than an infidel" (1 Timothy 5:8).

Whenever the husband is not the primary breadwinner in his marriage, this deficiency becomes a serious threat to his role of leadership and personal self-esteem. There are temporary exceptions to this, of course, particularly when by mutual consent the wife works as the husband take additional, specialized training. This is a wife's investment in their corporate good. But it should not be a permanent way of life. As a basic rule of thumb, the husband's income should provide food, shelter, and clothing. If the wife works, her job should be on a temporary basis for such things as house down payment, furniture, tuition for the children, or those cash purchases which the husband's income cannot provide. If her salary becomes a regular part of their living or is used to increase their standard of living it will usually be impossible for her ever to quit. The man needs the sense of responsibility that comes with knowing his family is dependent on him for the necessities of life. One of the dreadful abuses of welfare is that it becomes a way of life when unskilled men find it more profitable not to work—because their free government subsidy is greater than their earning capabilities. In the long run, such a subsidy is not "free" when given to the able-bodied, for it strips them of their manhood and self-respect. When that is gone, they have nothing.

The technology of our day has complicated man's role as provider. Unless he has waited to marry until he developed a skill or profession, he and his wife must often delay their family far longer than God intended to allow him time to do. The ever-present specter of inflation further complicates that problem by putting house buying beyond the reach of the average newlyweds. In spite of these and other serious problems today, a Christian man is likened to a "heretic" if he doesn't trust God to enable him to find some means of providing for his wife and children, if physically able to do so.

The Spirit-controlled family provider will not be a lazy man, nor will he be obsessed with materialism. Instead he will "seek first the Kingdom of God, and all these things will be added unto him" (*see* Matthew 6:33). Two things about that verse we must keep in mind. First, there is nothing wrong with a Christian man who is interested in business success. But when his interest in business overshadows his love for spiritual things, both he and the family are in trouble. Second, God will not supply him with everything on a silver platter without work. The divine command to Adam is still basic: Man is to earn his bread by the sweat of his face. Through the years I noticed that every time I asked God to supply a special need in our family's life, He did so—by giving me some extra work that brought in additional income. Rarely did His answer come like "manna from heaven."

Men are by nature extremists, and Satan will try to destroy them one way or the other—first by laziness. I have found some men who were content to float through life simply because they were lazy. For over a year I tried to help a forty-year-old father of four learn a profession. Finally, at the urging of some of my associates, we let him go. He frequently came in late, puttered unproductively, and was the first to leave in the evening. It simply cost us too much money to keep him. The difficult life to which he is needlessly subjecting his family is a carnal example of selfish laziness and is reprehensible for a Christian.

The second extreme is much more common: the Christian man who hides behind his work to avoid cultivating his spiritual life or that of his family. Workaholics are not Spirit-controlled; they are self-driven. One of the consistent traits of a Spirit-controlled husband and father is that, although he works hard and may occasionally endure heavy work-pressure periods, his work does not take priority over his family.

In this connection I have watched a few Christian men make the mistake of working every Sunday. One such manager of a supermarket made double-time pay for Sunday work and concluded that his family needed the money. He rarely came to church, though many times he assured me that he "loved the Lord." Naturally he experienced an underdeveloped spiritual life—and his home showed it. His three girls grew up with little interest in the things of the Lord, rarely attended church, and married unsaved men. I last saw him for counseling because his wife was running around with another man. I have to consider that an expensive price to pay for double-time wages.

I see nothing wrong with a Christian businessman working occasionally on Sunday. Even the Old Testament taught that when the ox fell into the ditch on the Sabbath, the farmer was to get him out, no matter how messy and muddy the task. But any Christian man who must work every Sunday—forcing him to absent himself consistently from the Lord's House—has the wrong job. I have seen men trust God for real miracles in this connection and find that He "always supplies our needs"! Happy is the man who understands that his vocation is a trust from God. His talents, energy, and creativity are gifts from God and should be used for His glory. No man has ever been shortchanged if he puts the Lord first vocationally.

The Husband as Father-Teacher

The first commandment God gave to Adam and Eve was to "Be fruitful, and multiply, and replenish the earth . . ." (Genesis 1:28). Since that time, fatherhood has played a major role in the life of the husband and has been a rich source of blessing to men who have taken this additional role seriously. In recent years, modern science has put into the hands of young couples birth-control techniques which enable them to limit the size of their family and, in a surprising number of cases, avoid having children altogether. Humanistically oriented educators' and population experts' warnings that we must reduce the size of our families have been so well received in America that the number of children per family dropped to 1.6 last year. This attitude is gaining popularity even among Christian families, in spite of the priority the Bible and Christianity have always placed on the family. The words of the Psalmist need to be pondered by every prospective parent: "Lo, children are an heritage of the Lord: and the fruit of the womb is his reward . . . . Happy is the man that hath his quiver full of them . . ." (Psalms 127:3, 5). An old Hebrew tradition tells us that a "quiver" which soldiers carried to war was large enough to contain five arrows. Could He be suggesting that, since children are such a blessing, a man would be fully happy with five of them?

Bev and I are somewhat biased on this subject because God gave us four children to raise, and one was lost prior to birth. We certainly can testify that children raised in the Lord are a blessing. God has showered us with far more blessings in our lives than we ever dreamed possible, but we have none that even come close to the treasures bearing our children's names—unless it is our five grandchildren. We are always saddened when we meet young couples who cheat themselves out of these greatest blessings of life. Almost anyone can propagate children, but raising them is a different matter. Fatherhood takes hard work, sacrifice, and time, but it is its own reward.

THE NATURE OF FATHERHOOD

The Spirit-controlled father does not lack specific instructions from the Word of God as to the true nature of his duties. Ephesians 6:4 states, "And, ye fathers, provoke not your children to wrath: but bring them up in the nurture and admonition of the Lord." There are three classic commands in this verse which we must consider individually.

1. Fathers are to love their children. "Provoke not your children to wrath." Every child needs love and intuitively seeks it from his parents. If his love is rejected or if Mom and Dad do not exhibit affection, he is filled with wrath. Anyone who studies the juvenile scene today, noting the hostility that emanates from teenagers and the high rate of rejection or negligence among their parents, must recognize that we are raising a generation of love-starved children.

When I did the research for *The Unhappy Gays: What Everyone Should Know About Homosexuality*, I was amazed to find that all homosexuals are filled with hostility. I have already acknowledged my own former problems with anger and have majored in counseling hostile married couples and individuals, so I think I know a little about Choleric wrath. But I have never seen anything like the homosexual brand of hostility. And what is the number-one cause? A rejecting father. One former homosexual, now a minister who is helping men come out of that unhappy lifestyle, said, "I have counseled over three hundred homosexuals and have yet to find one who experienced a good relationship with his father."

A juvenile-court judge, after presiding over thousands of juvenile cases, observed, "I have yet to see a boy come before my court who had a father who took him fishing or went to ball games or spent time with him." It has been my observation that the father who demonstrates his love for his children by making time for teaching them, no matter how busy his schedule, enjoys his children when they are adults. That doesn't mean they will never stir up a fuss and manifest their all-too-human nature. However, the wise man of Proverbs assures us that although "foolishness is bound up in the heart of the child," we can be certain that "the rod of correction shall drive it far from him" (Proverbs 22:15). Even the children of a loving, Spirit-controlled father may store a degree of foolishness in their hearts, which sooner or later will reveal itself in wrath. But their angry spirits will be much less severe and more short-lived than that of the child whose father has provoked him to wrath by neglecting to supply his need for love.

One of my dearest friends is a motorcycle nut. He has won almost every trophy a champion cycle racer can win. His garage contains more motorcycles than his house has people (and he is raising a large family). His oldest son was early introduced to a "dirt bike" (they never ride on the street for fear some fool driver will kill them) and together they have spent thousands of hours riding, repairing their machines, and planning the next Baja trip. But then the boy started running around with the wrong crowd and succeeded in getting himself kicked out of high school. Some tense months followed for two prayerfully concerned parents. The inevitable dope scene which forms a part of the public high schools in our community was drawing the lad into its orbit when suddenly—like the prodigal son—he came to himself. The father and the boy continued to ride and work on their bikes, and he wisely avoided nagging his son about his activities. Eventually, the teenager realized that Dad was the best friend he had on this earth. He re-dedicated his life to Christ, gave up his old friends, eventually married a lovely Christian girl, and today is industriously following his father in his construction business. Father love did it again!

2. Fathers are to teach their children.   If there is a consistent neglect among conscientious fathers today, it is in facing their responsibility as teachers of their children. Because Mother is the primary teacher during the first few years of a youngster's life, many men never assume their proper teaching role when the children get older. The Scripture clearly states: "Fathers, bring up your children in the nurture of the Lord." That is, train them by example and precept in the ways of God.

Children do not tell the truth by nature, nor do they automatically share or act responsibly. These are principles that must be instilled by example and precept. In addition, they must be taught skills commensurate with their age and sex. Unfortunately, the electronic advances of our age often create tools that are far too sophisticated for young boys in the learning stage. In the old days life was simple. A father only had a few tools, all of which his son could be taught to use at an early age. But today's power equipment presents special problems—yet they must learn, and Father is their best instructor. If he spends time teaching them skills, sports, and social customs, they will readily listen while he imparts to them the principles of character and the statutes of God.

3. Fathers are to discipline their children.   The hardest job in the whole business of fatherhood is discipline. Without it, however, there is no such thing as successful parenthood. We hear a great deal about "child abuse" today, as both the opinion molders of the media and federal bureaucrats have discovered one more "crisis" they can manipulate to trick the American people into succumbing to additional legislative interference in our personal lives. This one is more valid than the energy crisis, however, for as any hospital emergency-ward doctor will acknowledge, child abuse is on the increase. What would make an adult lash out and strike a helpless infant or child? The frustration of rage in an undisciplined person who has lost control. Usually the product of a rejecting or a permissive home, the parent cannot endure the pressure which endless crying or childish annoyance brings. Few child beaters are really murderers at heart, but all are selfish, angry, undisciplined people. They are almost as pathetic as the children they beat. However, as tragic as that kind of child abuse may be, another variety is far more common and less publicized. Consider carefully the children whose lives are destroyed through lack of parental discipline. Their number is legion! Most penitentiaries, juvenile halls, houses of correction, and cemeteries are full of them. Many others are borderline casualties who marry and divorce several times, father and abandon children, and are unable to keep a job. Such human tragedies could easily have been avoided had their fathers heeded the biblical injunction that a father who truly loves his son will "chasten" or discipline him.

Self-discipline, self-denial, and self-control are absolute essentials in maturing to adulthood. A father cannot possibly prepare his children educationally or vocationally for all the complex changes that await him in the twenty-first century. For instance, many present-day vocations will be automated out of existence. One thing a father can do for his children, however, is provide exactly what they need to prepare for whatever uncertainties lurk ahead—he can teach them discipline. The foundation for self-discipline is *parental* discipline. The child who is lovingly disciplined in the home will much more readily make the transition to self-discipline when he is older. The child raised without practical discipline is not only "provoked to wrath," but his lack of self-control contributes to his self-destruction or, at best, self-limitation.

Here at Christian Heritage College we readily see the difference. The most tragic waste of human talent and opportunity involves young people who lack sufficient self-discipline to be finishers. We teach our students that they shouldn't take all the easy courses, but rather try to select at least one difficult subject a year, for a passing grade in that class will build character—which is far more beneficial than knowledge. To be sure, knowledge is important, but character is far more so, because it determines what you do with what you know. No matter how much you know, nothing is more important than what you are. There is no substitute for Christian character, but waiting until you can send your child away to a Christian college, with the hope that the school will accomplish what you failed to achieve, is abdicating your role as a father.

Several years ago the Houston, Texas, police department published a list of *Twelve Rules for Raising Delinquent Children.* These rules verify that the police, who have to work with the products of permissiveness, were never de-ceived by the ivory-tower theorists and the trusting parents who believed the notion that children are born good and need to grow up expressing their goodness.

Twelve Rules for Raising Delinquent Children

1. Begin with infancy to give the child everything he wants. In this way he will grow up believing the world owes him a living.
2. When he picks up bad words, laugh at him. This will make him think he's cute. It will also encour-age him to pick up "cuter" phrases that will blow off the top of your head later.
3. Never give him any spiritual training. Wait till he is 21 and then let him "decide for himself."
4. Avoid use of the word "wrong." It may develop a guilt complex. This will condition him to believe later, when he is arrested for stealing a car, that society is against him and he is being persecuted.
5. Pick up everything he leaves lying around—books, shoes and clothing. Do everything for him so he will be experienced in throwing all responsibility onto others.
6. Let him read any printed matter he can get his hands on. Be careful that the silverware and drink-ing glasses are sterilized, but let his mind feast on garbage.
7. Quarrel frequently in the presence of your chil-dren. In this way they will not look shocked when the home is broken up later.

8. Give a child all the spending money he wants. Never let him earn his own. Why should he have things as tough as YOU had them?
9. Satisfy his every craving for food, drink and comfort. See that every sensual desire is gratified. Denial may lead to harmful frustration.
10. Take his part against neighbors, teachers and policemen. They are all prejudiced against your child.
11. When he gets into real trouble, apologize for yourself by saying, "I never could do anything with him."
12. Prepare for a life of grief. You will be apt to have it.

The techniques of child raising were covered quite thoroughly by Bev in *How to Develop Your Child's Temperament*, where she applies the biblical principles of discipline not only to the four temperaments but to the various ages of children and teens, so we shall not repeat them here. But it is important, Dad, to point out two final principles about fathering. First, it is your responsibility from God to see that your children are well disciplined. Your wife may do it when they are small or when you're away, but you should see to it they are disciplined in love. Second, you must be an example of what you teach! Nothing turns young people off faster than hypocrisy—and teaching one thing while doing another qualifies as hypocrisy.

While attending a social activity in the home of one of my associate pastors recently, I happened to be within easy earshot when his teenage son answered the phone. He told the party on the other end that his father was busy and couldn't come to the phone, but the caller persisted. To his credit, he was equally persistent and politely offered to take the number and have his father call later. As he hung up the phone, his friend said, "Why didn't you just tell them he wasn't home and avoid all that hassle?" The teen replied, "My father wouldn't like that; it isn't true." That boy will never have to take a course in basic honesty!

WHAT WILL YOUR CHILDREN SAY?

Sixteen Christians attending a home Bible study were asked the question, "What was your father?" One said, "He was a loving, tender guy." Another commented that her dad was a dedicated Christian who loved her very much. Some reported they "never really knew" their dad, and so on around the group. Not one mentioned his father's profession, possessions, or position in life! If the Lord tarries and you depart this life before your family, what will they say about you? You aren't impressing them with what you do for a living, but by what you are. Who are you?

The Husband as Family Priest

The most neglected role of the husband is one that predominated in ancient days—that of family priest. In Ephesians 5 we are told that the husband is to the wife what Christ is to the church. If Christ is our High Priest, then, husband, you are the priest of your home. All spiritual instruction is your responsibility.

You are doubtless aware that in many homes the mother takes care of the religious training of the children, which she can pursue during their early years. If the father has no interest in spiritual things when they reach their teens, the spiritual mortality rate is extremely high.

When your wife conceived the children who bear your name, more was brought into this world than mind, emotions, and body. People are uniquely different from animals, for they possess a distinct spiritual side to their nature which needs cultivation by training and exercise. Far too many Christian fathers think they have fulfilled their responsibility by providing food, shelter, love, and discipline for their children. But this would neglect the spiritual potential of both the wife and children. It is your responsibility to lead them in the paths of the Lord. Consider the following ways a father fulfills his family priesthood.

1. He will be a Spirit-controlled man.   This, of course, is the foundation of the Christian father's priesthood, as it is in every other role.

2. He will be regular in his daily Bible reading.   We have found that children who see their father feed daily on the Word of God and incorporate its teachings into his life are easily taught this daily practice in their youth. More is "caught" in this area than "taught."

3. He will lead in family devotions.   It would seem incredible to me that any Spirit-controlled family would not spend some time each day in Bible reading and prayer. We found it best to tailor the devotional time to the age of the children. When they were small, we read a short passage of Scripture, taught one of them to pray, and then closed the session with prayer. As they grew older, we enlarged the Scripture reading and let them take part. In their junior and teen years, we would often discuss the scriptural passage and have at least three participate in prayer. Today you may wish to make use of the excellent devotional helps and materials available in Christian bookstores. They also carry exciting children's stories that maintain the interest of toddlers. We found these to be excellent for story time during the evening or just before bedtime.

My pastor friend Dr. Truman Dollar, of the Kansas City Baptist Temple, has a devotional system that may be even

better than the one we used. Every night the family has
devotions together just before the children go to bed. Dad
leads when home; if he's away, his wife, Donna, leads in
Bible reading and prayer. If both parents are away, their
oldest son, Tim, leads. When he is gone the next oldest is in
charge. All baby-sitters are instructed in the procedure, so
that every night ends in family prayer. If our children were
still home we would try this procedure.

The family prayer and Bible reading time, often called
"the family altar" or "family devotions" can best be led by
Dad. He has the more commanding voice, and it is good for
the children to know that Dad is 100 percent behind a program of building spirituality into the lives of children. I had
the joy of seeing what I call a "Texas wastrel" (a man who
had wasted his life on the sins of the flesh) come to Christ.
Sometime after his conversion we were discussing why he
came to a minister while half-drunk and obviously on the
bottom rung of life. "It was the old family Bible my father
read from each night. I turned my back on my father's faith,
but I always knew it was available if I ever got desperate."
That kind of confidence has stood many a child in good
stead when tempted by sin, philosophy, and materialism. It
is the father-priest of the home who should lead in such
devotional times. Admittedly, some temperaments find it
harder to conduct such sessions than others. Your family,
however, doesn't need a polished speaker at that moment,
but the priestly leadership in Bible reading and prayer by
the most important person in their lives. It isn't how you do
it that is important; it's who you are.

PRACTICAL SUGGESTIONS FOR THE DEVOTIONAL HOUR

To make those devotional times as effective as possible,
we offer the following suggestions:

1. Plan a time that best fits the schedule of your family. This may change as your children grow or when Dad has to work a different shift. But there should be one special time when the family can include that ten-to-thirty-minute family session in their program. We found that right after the evening meal was usually the best time. Everyone was relaxed and in a good mood to talk to God.

2. Be consistent but not legalistic. Occasionally an important Little League game will be missed unless you skip devotions, but as a rule, at least five nights a week should find the family sharing their devotional time together.

3. It takes cooperation from both Mother and Dad for this program to be consistent. Mother must start the meal on time so it doesn't run into other scheduled activities. (Many a Christian wife grumbles at her husband's inconsistency, without realizing that the lateness of the evening meal often contributes to the devotional neglect). Dad should gather the Bible and/or devotional materials and mentally prepare for devotions, perhaps reading over the Bible portion before dinner.

4. Encourage the children to take part. Father doesn't have to read the Scripture and direct the session every time, but the children should understand what has been read.

5. Use this time to teach the family to pray. Like many families, we installed a cork bulletin board on our kitchen wall and posted a world map pinpointing the missionaries our church supports. To this we added others who had visited our home and our special requests for prayer. It was always a blessing to the children to formally thank God for His answer when it came, at which time we removed the request from the board.

Praying comes easily for children when, as far back as they can remember, grace was said at each meal—and talking to Jesus became as natural as talking to anyone else.

Our own children still have no difficulty expecting God's answers to prayer, for they traced His faithfulness to our family many times. One occasion comes to mind. I have always believed in sharing our needs with the family and, whenever possible, visualizing our request to make it more specific. Our car was about to gasp its last breath, so we discussed buying a new one. We all decided that our family of six needed a nine-passenger station wagon. We even picked out a three-seated Plymouth which featured a special door and electronic window. Naturally it had to feature an automatic transmission and all the "extras." By the time we added the requirements together, the car was far too expensive for our meager budget, so we began to ask God for a good used one. When I found a beautiful picture in a magazine of just what we wanted, we cut it out and pinned it on our prayer board. Each night the children remembered to pray for the car. Frankly, at times their faith was stronger than mine, because that model car was less than a year old and used ones were as scarce as a hen's teeth. One evening the phone rang. A Navy chief who attended another church in our city heard we were looking for a good used car and called to ask us if we would like to buy his. He was being sent overseas and had this "seven-month-old Plymouth station wagon"! I was almost too nervous to ask if it was a nine-passenger model with three seats, but of course it was. We bought the car by taking over his payments, the best car buy we ever made. That car transported our family for over five years and remains the one car that stands out in the children's minds to this day. Two of them are married, with children of their own, and both have cars they prayed into their families. We taught our children to pray about everything from clothes to houses. We also taught them Scripture verses like: "Hitherto have ye asked nothing in my name: ask, and ye shall receive, that your joy may be full" (John 16:24).

The father-priest who faithfully fulfills his spiritual responsibilities to his family lives to enjoy his children later in life. Doubtless you know many who wish they could experience those young, pliable years all over again, but once passed they are gone forever. The father-priest who does his work faithfully fashions a spiritual belt of protection that will protect his children all through life. The priestly ministry of father is a reinforcement every family needs to assure the successful raising of their children.

The Husband as Family Protector

As far back as anthropologists go in their research, man has always been the protector of his family. When we were in Africa last year, we saw a typical native scene, a small village of five huts, all surrounded by a handmade wall with only one gate. As we stepped inside, there sat the father, bow across his lap, obviously protecting the homes of his five wives and twenty-nine children.

The need for physical protection varies with the community and the man's means and opportunity. It is so basically understood in our society that we need only mention some of the less obvious but equally important areas in which a husband is the family protector.

1. He will protect his wife psychologically. We have already seen that self-acceptance and self-respect are essential to every human being. What you think of yourself influences everything you do. In fact, what you think of yourself is far more important than what you suppose other people think of you. To a wife, her husband's opinion of her is of vital importance. For if he approved of her, it matters little who does not; but if he does not esteem her, it doesn't matter who else does.

Every wise husband will go out of his way, as we saw in

our study of love, to encourage his wife with his approval. The Bible says a husband should "honor the wife as the weaker vessel" (*see* 1 Peter 3:7). You have no doubt seen a man publicly humiliate his wife in front of mutual friends by sarcastically announcing her weaknesses, or by subjecting her to other forms of ill-advised ridicule. Sanguine men do it because they are tactless and egocentric; consequently, they will say anything to get a laugh. Melancholies criticize everything and everyone (unless they're filled with the Spirit), so their wives are no exception. No one can be more sarcastic than a Choleric. He often has the mistaken idea that hanging his wife's undesirable traits out to dry before his friends may induce her to "shape up." Of all the temperaments, Phlegmatics are least likely to criticize their wives in public, but they also are seldom heard to say something complimentary.

A MELCHLOR husband came in for counseling several times. He was both critical and sarcastic (a devastating formula for ruining a wife), but he knew he should change. According to his official report, his SANPHLEG little wife "did everything wrong." As a highly successful businessman who ran a very efficient office (with the aid of a secretary who could put up with him in short doses), he could not understand why his wife failed to do the same at home. He confessed, however, that his way of dealing with the situation was making matters worse. You guessed it—his management technique required him to criticize her from the moment he came in from work until they went to bed. "You don't keep the house straight." "The kitchen is disorganized." "The family records are a disaster." "You ruin the gas dryer by never cleaning the lint remover." "You can't even fold my socks right." To no one's surprise, their love life had dipped to zero. I asked him if he had ever tried *praise.*

"Of course not," came the reply. "I never have anything to praise her for!"

"Has your wife ever been unfaithful?"

"No," he answered.

"Let's start there." Further questioning supplied the following information—she had borne him three children, served fairly good meals, was a dedicated Christian, loved and was good to his mother, dressed his kids well and helped them with their homework. "But she is such a messy housekeeper!" he interjected. His tunnel vision could only focus on this glaring weakness, making him impervious to the fact that his criticism, nagging, and harping were only making things worse. Fortunately, in his desperate straits he was willing to try anything—even praise.

We worked out a plan that called for thirty days of praise. It took all the self-control he could muster, but he fulfilled his assignment and then furnished this report: "The first four days she didn't know what to expect, but gradually she relaxed. On the fifth day she met me at the door with a kiss, which she hadn't done in years. She started cooking my favorite foods again and actually put my laundry in the drawer before I got home. Last week some gal loaned her a book called *The Total Woman,* and one night, when the kids were at my mother's, you wouldn't believe how she met me at the door!" He never mentioned whether her housekeeping was improving (it probably was), but somehow I don't think he cared anymore.

One of the secondary meanings for the biblical word *submission* involves being "responsive" or "a responder." A woman is a responder to her husband's treatment. I have never seen a woman fail to respond affirmatively to love, kindness, and praise.

2. He will protect his children psychologically. No man looms more important in the heart of children than their father. Consequently, what he thinks of them is of paramount significance in their formative years. It is essential that fathers learn to gear down to the level of the child's character and encourage or praise him in all that he does. Like a wife, children respond positively to praise but never to criticism.

When we returned from our missionary tour of the world, our son Larry and his loving wife, Kathy, were living in our home with their two boys, ages one and three, while awaiting the completion of their new home. First they were promised the house in two months, then two more . . . and so far we have lived together for nine delightful months. This association has afforded an unusual opportunity to watch two of our grandchildren and review some of the principles of child raising. And it has been interesting to watch Larry deal with his boys. I certainly wish I had known some of those principles when he was their age! With one encouraging word from him, his boys will try anything, no matter how fruitless their initial efforts. Anytime they attempt something that is beyond their capability, they look immediately to him for approval. Noting that look in their eyes, I again began to perceive that all children look to Dad for his approval and praise. Most of the psychologically shell-shocked people I have counseled never enjoyed that kind of approval as children. Almost all negative thinking patterns about oneself begin in childhood. A thoughtful father is a marvelous antidote.

3. He will protect his family from philosophical error. The world in which we live is engaged in a battle for control of the human mind, and every Christian father ought to be aware of this. God is using the Bible, the church, and the home to build into the minds of our children those principles they need to enable them to live properly in this life and eternity. Satan, on the other hand, uses everything at his disposal to corrupt the minds of our children and to inflame their youthful passions in order to wrest them from the plan and purpose of God. He has seized our once-great school system and now uses it to propagate atheism, evolution, amorality, free love, debilitating drugs and unbelievably evil philosophies. He also has appropriated TV, movies, books, magazines, and other media that reach into the mind. The Spirit-filled father will recognize these prime sources of evil and keep them out of his house. Since children will not instinctively exercise good judgment and seem to be mesmerized by that which is harmful, God gave them parents to govern their decisions. A few years ago naive parents used to argue with me when I suggested that they censor the TV in their home. The tube has become so corrupt and degenerate that parents no longer deny its effect. Hollywood's exaltation of immorality, lesbianism, and male homosexuality has revealed it for the entertainment corrupter it has always been. "Man's ways are not God's ways," and Christian parents ought to face it. We cannot trust Satan to entertain or educate our family.

Recently my pastor friend Jim Reimer, of the First Baptist Church of Enid, Oklahoma, invited Bill Kelly (the superintendent of our Christian school system here in San Diego) and me to speak in his church on a Wednesday evening in an attempt to encourage his congregation to begin a Christian school in the community. He asked me privately if it was appropriate for him to be motivated because of his concern for the influence of secular education upon his own children. I laughed and then explained, "That is exactly why we started Christian High School of San Diego fifteen years ago. I was concerned about the evil philosophy my children were exposed to at school, day after day." Jim didn't realize it, but he was revealing that he had his priorities straight; he is a father first and a pastor second. Every father ought to be concerned about the kind of education his children are receiving. If it exercises an unwholesome influence on them (and it probably does, now that the federal government controls our local schools through federal funding), he ought to do everything within his power to provide his children with a Christian education. I am convinced that every Bible-believing church in America ought to consider using its facilities for a weekday Christian school. According to the latest local education tests, we do a far better job of education than the public school, and our children are safer from physical, moral, and philosophical harm. In addition, we can teach them the Bible. Churches without adequate facilities to provide more than one or two classrooms ought to cooperate with other churches of like mind.

What about the expense of private education? With most parents this is a vital factor. But God has promised He will provide all our needs, and if you recognize this as a need and make it an earnest matter of prayer, God will supply the means. Many of the parents who send their children to our schools (and there are almost 2,000 now in K–12) thought they could never afford it, but God has provided miracle after miracle. Never limit God through unbelief, by deciding in advance what He cannot do. That's why the children of Israel spent forty years in the desert unnecessarily.

4. He will protect his wife and children from disrespect. The rebellion that lurks in the heart of all children will ultimately surface in the home. That rebellion usually takes its first form in disrespect toward their mother. When children are small, minor insubordination will be treated as disobedience by Mom, but if not squelched early, it becomes a habit that only the father can cure. If he does not, that disrespect will eventually be turned on him, then directed outside the home, and finally pit the child against society and the police. Rarely do police officers have to arrest respectful children.

No one but the father can guarantee that the children of the home will respect their mother—provided he speaks respectfully of her himself. I have raised my children that way. To this day, my sons, who are very fond of their mother and always relaxed around her, may tease her but they are never disrespectful.

The husband who loves the Lord and his wife will guarantee her that respect. The Lord requires it when he says, "Husband, give honor unto your wife as the weaker vessel . . . that your prayers be not hindered" (*see* 1 Peter 3:7).

7

The Art of Family Communication

Communication is a basic part of all human life. It is one of the significant differences separating people from animals. Man has an innate desire for communication with both God and his fellowman. Many individuals substitute communicating with their fellow humans for communication with God. Ultimately, this is self-destructive because it tends to be communication for selfish purposes. Individuals who genuinely enjoy communication with God through the power of His indwelling Spirit will be more relaxed about themselves and others, and consequently they find it easier to communicate with those around them.

The experts in communication point out that this art contains three basic elements: (1) talking; (2) listening; and (3) understanding. We could add two more important ingredients: body signs and empathy. Everyone knows how to define talking, but *talking* does not guarantee communication. As Dr. Howard Hendricks has often said at our seminars, "Talking is easy; anyone can do it. But communication is hard work." And we could add that communication requires two people, both concentrating on the same thing:

that which is being said. Because talking is so much easier than listening, the hardest problem in the whole process is listening. If the listener isn't interested in the subject and has no motivation to pay attention, communication is almost impossible. As a public speaker I have long assumed that communication is the responsibility of the speaker. But after teaching on both the high school and college level for years, I finally came to realize that the best visualized presentation (with printouts included) will not be understood without the cooperation of the listener. If that is true generally, it is even more so in a family situation. Communication always requires at least two people.

One of the most advertised problems in marriage is that of communication breakdown. If active marriage counselors were polled, the top two problems would be family finances and communication—and though they may differ on which is number one, most would rate one of them first and the other second. One expert suggests that 50 percent of all marriages have a serious communication problem. And Christians are not exempt. Recently Bev and I counseled an active church couple with several children. One of their illustrations was that the wife had driven off on Sunday evening without asking if he wanted to attend the choir's performance of the cantata in which she was singing. He was upset because she hadn't asked his desire but assumed he didn't wish to attend, and he angrily said, "I always attend Sunday-night services!" Communication was so painful for this couple that both had avoided sharing their true feelings.

Gradual Communication Difficulties

It has long been a phenomenon in marriage counseling that couples who never have a difficult time communicating before marriage can develop such communication difficulties afterward. Even couples who maintain, "We still love each other deeply!" can find communication difficult. Before marriage they could talk endlessly about everything (particularly on the phone while the girl's father is trying to call home), but gradually after marriage it becomes more difficult until it becomes an apparent problem. How did it happen?—"Very gradually." The following are some of the things that slowly stifle conversation between two lovebirds after the honeymoon.

1. Differing perspectives. Prior to marriage, the couple shared a common dream, the ultimate marriage and home. After marriage, the young man is faced with new responsibilities and restrictions that cause him to concentrate on supporting his wife, and sometimes he even questions whether or not it's worth it in the light of these restrictions. At twenty or so years of age he had finally earned the right to come and go in his home or apartment without having to give an account of his time or activities. Suddenly he's confronted with a wife who wants to know: "When will you be home . . . where will you be . . . who are you going out with?" Very gradually the novelty of married life is replaced by a feeling of irritation at this new requirement of accountability.

Vocationally, the husband begins to shift into a higher gear than during the courtship days. Then he had somewhat sidestepped his vocational interests (not the work or—in the case of the student—his studies; but they were not number one in his mind—getting married was). Now he returns to a basic need, vocational aptitude and financial solvency. Prior to marriage their number-one interest was shared equally. Now he goes off alone into a different world. She may ask, "How did it go at school [or work] today?'' and he may give a five- or ten-minute answer; but he spent eight to ten hours of his life at it, apart from her.

The wife, if she does not work, becomes domesticated in her thinking, concentrating on meals, clothes, house, and so on. If she divides herself between vocational and domesticated thoughts, the young bride also may be somewhat disillusioned at the realities of marriage. Rushing home from work to plan meals, instead of eating mother's cooking, takes getting used to. It is not uncommon for two lovers to sit at home in silence within weeks after the wedding, both silently questioning the rightness of their decision but unwilling to discuss their true feelings. This adjustment period is usually temporary and is the initial phase of adjustment. It is important that they talk honestly and freely during these days; but it's not easy.

2. Different primary interests and involvements.   It is natural for a young married woman to begin thinking of motherhood. As she does, and particularly after becoming pregnant, her number-one interest is the baby (and the home). His number-one concern is increasingly vocational, especially if they are taking on the additional responsibilities of parenthood. As such, the books and magazines he reads are vocational; hers are family centered. Her thoughts become immediate, his increasingly long-range. While she is thinking of ''bassinets and buntings,'' he is thinking of ''a place in the suburbs.'' They begin to put priorities on different things. She may feel that his reluctance to spend money for the nursery shows a disinterest in the baby. If she verbalizes such an idea, he may become offended. He is apt to feel that her desire to buy furniture for the baby now is unreasonable in the light of saving for a down payment on their new home. Different marital priorities produce conflicts of interest.

One of the reasons we favor the Lamaze birth program, becoming so popular today, is that it forces the couple to prepare *together* for the baby's arrival. It affords them a vital interest to share something intimately at a time when they need something to share. Unfortunately, hospitals indicate that many husbands are difficult to persuade to take the training. This mutual interest, though valuable, is often short-lived. They need other areas of interest to share.

A deep marital companionship and friendship must be built on mutual interests. Whenever I see a husband and wife who do not share common goals and interests, I look for trouble. If all they share is the same name, house, bed, and children, they will gradually grow apart. They must develop common interests. That is where the church and mutual spiritual interests greatly aid the Spirit-controlled couple. A regular study of the Word, Christian friends, and other Christ-related activities are a real asset.

A woman, particularly in the early days of marriage, would be wise to learn as much as possible about her husband's work, his favorite sports, and the daily news, if those are his chief areas of interest. It is a wise husband who also cultivates his wife's interests and keeps up with her reading levels. One of the reasons seminaries have special classes for "seminary wives" is that so many couples have such a diversity of interests during the husband's three years in school—because the wife is not studying the Bible along with her husband.

Another factor in this connection is friends. Unless they are strong Christians, couples are apt to make new friendships with others who are not interested in spiritual things. The young wife, confined to the home and usually without transportation, has to make friends in her apartment or neighborhood. The husband makes new friends in his changing classes at school or at work. Consequently, it is not uncommon for the former "inseparables" to desire different nights out with their work or neighborhood associates. This can be dangerous.

3. Opposite temperaments affect communication. Temperament influences everything in a person's life, particularly conversation. What appears clever and cute before marriage may appear irritating afterward. Sanguines are supertalkers. Their motto is: "When in doubt, talk," or as a Sanguine friend of mine said, "Sanguines enter a room mouth first!" That is only true when they have an audience to perform for. Prior to marriage, they go into their act for their "intended." After they have said everything they know three times, they begin to be silent until a visitor arrives. That makes the spouse resentful that a Sanguine "talks more when a stranger is here than when we are alone."

Cholerics talk continuously about business, are opinionated, and often thrive on argumentation. It is difficult to talk to a Choleric. If you disagree, he baits you into verbal argument. If you concur, there isn't much to say which he hasn't already stated. Warning: Disagree with a Choleric at your own risk! No one can be more sarcastic and caustic.

Melancholies are verbal perfectionists with a built-in obsession to be precise and to correct everyone else's way of doing things. They take disagreement extremely personal and often read into what you say exactly what you *meant* but didn't want to say (and sometimes what you don't mean).

Phlegmatics are not supertalkers. They let others speak, evaluate the whole scene, and rarely disagree, for fear of criticism or conflict. Fortunately, they are extremely diplomatic. Were it not for that, their partner might have them in a verbal confrontation all the time.

These temperament differences only expose the vast thinking differences which most couples possess. There is a need to learn to see life through the partner's eyes.

4. One- or two-celled thinking patterns affect communication. Another subtle difference between couples in marriage is the ability to think of more than one thing at a time. Bev has the ability to carry on eight things at once. Not me—I can think of only one subject at a time. I came home one night to find her caring for our grandchildren who had Tupperware all over the floor. She had a cake in the oven, was cooking something on the stove, and while setting the table had the telephone nestled against her ear listening to an endless conversation. As I went by she whispered, "Hi!" and puckered up for a kiss. I can't do that. When you talk to me on the phone you either get my undivided attention or nothing.

This characteristic is probably more a result of differences in temperament than in sexual identity. Usually men are considered more single-celled in their thinking, but I'm not sure that is true. We have an attorney friend who reads legal briefs while watching TV. Bev can do that, but neither his wife nor I can. Bev used to get annoyed at me because I wouldn't talk to her during a TV program. I can't do it. In fact, I don't even hear her. Many couples are opposite in this regard.

You can imagine what this does to communication when one wants to talk and cannot get the attention of the other. What often happens is the one seeking to gain attention gets louder and louder, and the other tunes him out even more or gets annoyed.

This is not a fatal problem, once both partners understand it and work on it. We have found that, instead of letting it become a source of irritation, it can provoke humor. To this day, Bev or the children will react to my lack of attention to their conversations with, "Hi, wall! How are the wife and kids?" If I hear it, we all laugh; if not, I awake from my fog—aware I am the object of their fun.

5. *Unresolved differences produce conflicts.* Most couples find after the honeymoon that they have far more temperament, background, and personal differences than they ever dreamed possible. These differences must be brought out through communication and discussed openly. Eventually, a plan of operation involving change for one—or compromise for both—is essential. Otherwise it will ultimately prove disastrous when such differences produce a clash of wills.

A ridiculous illustration of this occurred during our second year of marriage. We lived in two rooms of a sixteen-room southern mansion while attending college, in exchange for my doing the yard work. One beautiful evening we had a lovely dinner on the patio while the owners were away. It was a delightful setting, but we ruined it. Bev was about three months' pregnant with our first child, so I suggested she should drink her milk. (Every prospective father knows unborn babies need the calcium which milk provides.) Bev said, "I don't drink milk." Frankly, I thought that was stupid. I thought everyone drank milk, particularly an expectant mother. So I urged tactfully; she refused. I tried forcefully and threateningly; she still refused. Finally I said, "Honey, if you don't drink that milk, I'm going to pour it on your head!" to which she replied, "Then you'd better pour it, because I'm not drinking that milk." You just don't tell a twenty-two-year-old carnal Choleric that you're not going to do something! So I stupidly poured it on her head. It destroyed communication at our house for two days, not to mention ruining what could have been a lovely evening. Twenty-nine years later, all I can think of to describe that scene is the literary gem "What fools these mortals be"!

Weapons That Destroy Communication

Self-preservation is the well-advertised first law of life— as true psychologically as it is physically. Dr. Henry Brandt says, "There is no nakedness comparable to psychological nakedness." All of us employ weapons to protect ourselves from exposure. The problem with their use is that they stifle communication. Consider them carefully; they are to be avoided.

1. Explosion. A very effective tool for self-defense, and the one most commonly used at home, is an angry explosion. This engenders an argumentative spirit and invariably does more damage than good. Explosion teaches a partner that we have a limit on how far we can be pushed, automatically closing ourselves off to communication in that area. We spent ample time on this in chapter 4 so that it does not warrant repetition, except to say that Spirit-controlled family members do not use this tool—or they cease being Spirit-controlled.

2. Tears. Next to explosion, and often as a result of it, tears are the most popular of psychological weapons to defend ourselves. Naturally, it is more popular with women than with men and is very effective in saying, "If you push me too far, I'll cry." Once the dam breaks into a flood of tears, conversation comes to a screeching halt, unless the attacker is so insensitive that he ruthlessly lashes out in spite of them.

3. Criticism. It takes an extremely mature person to accept disagreement, criticism, or opposition without being defensive. The natural inclination (though not a very spiritual reaction) is to criticize the other person. Some forceful types soon learn they can keep their partners off-balance and under threat of critical attack, and thus force him or her to avoid bringing up anything unpleasant or distasteful. This may stifle communication, but it does nothing for love. One dominant, compulsive wife castigated her husband verbally from the time he came in until he left. She would rip the newspaper from his hands, constantly telling and retelling whatever bothered her (for as far back as courtship, thirty-five years before). One day she talked to him endlessly through the bathroom door and finally burst in on him, thinking he wasn't listening. This man used to drive aimlessly around the city in his car, just dreading going home. Talking may be a relief valve to the talker, but it certainly is no relief to the hearer.

4. Silence. Phlegmatics and some Melancholies have found silence a great tool in avoiding the unpleasant. Whether it is avoiding an argument by silence (through hiding behind the newspaper or slinking off into the bathroom or garage), it is an aggravating weapon to the one it is used upon. The extroverted temperaments find it all but impossible to use silence as a weapon. Sanguines can't be silent more than thirty seconds at a time, and Cholerics are not much better.

The weapon of silence usually takes two forms: retreat or resentment. Those who retreat into a self-protective shell are telling their opponent (or partner) that if they push too hard, they will pull "the turtle act" and pop their head inside a shell, cutting off all communication. Those who use silence out of resentment are really angry people.

A Phlegmatic man whose slow speech made him no match for his CHLORSAN wife (who could talk like a

machine gun running wide open) told me, "I've finally discovered how to handle that woman!" When I inquired as to
his new technique he replied, "Silence! She can't stand it!
Last week I went five days without saying a word to her." I
warned him that ultimately that kind of angry resentment
would give him ulcers. He laughed and said, "I'm a Phlegmatic; they don't get ulcers." Little did either of us dream
that in two weeks he would have to be rushed to the hospital with just such a malady, at twenty-eight years of age.

The longest I have known anyone to be silent toward a
spouse through anger was twenty-one days. And, believe it
or not, they were both extremely dedicated Christian workers. She was a CHLORSAN who made snap judgments and
he was a PHLEGMEL scholar who was extremely deliberate.
She talked nine-tenths of their marriage, made most decisions, and out-argued him during every debate or discussion. He finally resorted to silence until she would shut up
and let him say what was really in his heart. It was incredible to me that two people could be married for thirty years
and have to resort to such weapons in order to live together.
She had to "study to be quiet," and he had to repent of his
anger.

5. Endless chatter. Some people can't stand silence. It is
almost as though they fear that silence will provide the partner and family with an opportunity to ask some devastating
question that might expose their weaknesses. So they talk
and talk and talk. I've met people who (I felt certain) must
talk in their sleep, because it obviously took no conscious
thought to direct their tongue. Consequently, they chatter
endlessly about nothing. Usually this is a sign of an extremely insecure person (although some are like the
dominant, compulsive person mentioned under "Criticism"). Such individuals are dreadfully afraid of exposure,

unaware they *are* exposing themselves. Some women seem to tend to this loquacious life-style more than men, although I have seen my share of male supertalkers also. The husband of such a talker was meeting with me regularly and had really learned to walk in the Spirit. One day he came in for his appointment with a smile, to tell what he had done the night before. It seemed that his wife had been running off at the mouth for almost an hour when he got up, walked to her side, and gently placed his hand over her mouth and said, "Sweetheart, I love you; I love you; I love you—but my ears need a rest!" They both laughed and gradually she is learning to slow down her torrent of words.

There are other weapons which people use to stifle true communication, but these are the most common. If you find yourself using them, trust God for victory, that you might enjoy the "love and sound mind" He wants to give to you and your partner.

Nine Keys to Effective Communication

Like almost everything else, effective communication is an art that must be cultivated by two people. In this case it is both the listener as well as the speaker. The following nine suggestions are keys to better family communication and are designed to ease those special issues that must be dealt with by head-to-head communication.

1. Learn to understand your partner. Getting to know another person thoroughly is not a simple feat, and it certainly cannot be done before marriage. Most couples live together many years before they really understand each other. One of the reasons is that they are both so wrapped up in themselves that they married for the wrong reason. They had in mind that their partner would understand them.

It is amazing how many people are obsessed with the desire that their partner understand them, when in reality they should be more concerned with understanding their partner.

A noted family counselor said, "If your supreme desire is to be understood, you are a sick person." The whole thrust of the Gospel is to "give" as Christ gave to us. One of the basic signs of a selfish person is that he is not interested in understanding and accepting others, but desires that they should accept and understand *him*. The best tool known for helping you learn to understand your partner is the temperament theory. It explains "actions and reactions" in such a way that it takes the sting out of why your partner acts as he does. Many a source of irritation is resolved when, for example, it becomes apparent that a tendency to talk is a reflection of a Sanguine nature, or that a partner's exasperating analytical scrutiny is an outgrowth of his Melancholy temperament. Add to this the differences in the sexes, backgrounds, and values—and you will see that it takes a good deal of time to really learn to understand one's partner. When, however, that time comes, it removes considerable heat from their relationship at those times when their differences come into conflict.

2. Accept your partner unconditionally and cheerfully. Everyone fears rejection, some temperaments more than others, but the more we love someone, the greater is our desire for his or her acceptance. And because we all communicate by "emotion" as well as speaking, it is imperative that couples truly accept each other so that they will sincerely emote that acceptance. This is particularly true when some difficulties or problem area in the marriage must be discussed. Like understanding, the assurance of acceptance removes heat from a potentially difficult situation, while the fear of rejection is like pouring gasoline on a fire.

Both of the above steps are basic and should be continually cultivated throughout a marriage, not just at pressure times. When they are, it softens the times when issues and differences must be dealt with head-on.

3. Plan a suitable time for your partner. Most communication sessions are instigated by one of the members of the family, usually one of the partners. We have already seen that some partners are sharp in the morning; they are called "robins." The "owls" are just the opposite; they wake up slowly but are often night people. Obviously, it is best to pick a time that is best suited to your partner. A good rule to follow in this regard is: Never talk about money or "heavy" problems after 9:30 or 10:00 P.M. Somehow, all problems look darker and loom larger at night.

Learning to understand your partner makes it easier to schedule the best time for a communication session. With most men, it is after dinner when devotions are complete. Sometimes couples have to go out for dinner to assure privacy from the children. Communication sessions are not limited to the parents; sometimes the teenagers initiate such a session. I recall that one of ours called us into a meeting to point out he did not think the rest of the family treated one of his friends properly. Suddenly the reason came out: "Why should we? The guy's a real jerk!" said one of the teens. As you can imagine, we had a lively discussion. The thrust of it was that one young person felt sorry for this neglected kid; his brother and sisters didn't like him. As soon as he conveyed his concern for the other teen, we all found it easier to understand his motives and pledged to be more polite to his friend. Such open confrontation is healthy.

4. Introduce the subject tactfully.   The more difficult the subject, the more tactfully it should be presented. Most couples learn little techniques that after a while signal a "heavy" communication session. Whenever Bev says, "Honey, can I share something with you?" I get a good grip on my fractured ego—I know "it" is coming. When I say to her, "Honey, are you in a good mood tonight?" she turns a little green around the gills and prepares for that moment of truth. Sometimes your partner may not feel up to facing one of his weaknesses or problem areas. Be prepared to delay the session, remembering you're more interested in maintaining a lasting relationship than in clinging to some particular issue.

5. Speak the truth in love. (Ephesians 4:15).   Lovingly share how you feel and how you assess the situation or the problem or what bugs you. Say it simply, truthfully, but always lovingly. For although love never dilutes the truth, neither does it inflict unnecessary injury.

Truth is sharp and it may hurt. For example, when a wife informs her husband she thinks he ought to put his own socks in the hamper or use better table manners—or the husband suggests the wife may be more tolerant with one child than she is with another, or that she has been getting careless with the housework, or whatever—it will hurt; truth usually does. But such communication is like my surgeon friend, who can't help people without hurting them. Because he loves his patients, however, he never makes his incisions greater than necessary.

6. Allow for reaction time.   It would be ideal if we were all so mature that our response to being confronted with a serious weakness or flaw in our makeup would be to thank the person who shared the truth. But who is really that ideal? Only the Spirit-controlled man or woman! Most others will become defensive and react accordingly. Some may resort to one or more of the weapons for self-defense given above. You had better be ready with a calm spirit to take anything they offer. For if you react to their reaction, you have ruined the session. And the responsibility for peace is on you, since you knew in advance what you were going to say and could prepare for it. However, your partner is usually taken by surprise. Actually, you can trust God to be ready with a "soft answer," for as we have seen, it turns away wrath. By giving a soft answer: "We'll think about it," or "I hope I haven't hurt you, but that is how it seemed to me," you can often make your point.

7. *Never argue or defend yourself.* Squelch the desire to defend your position and, unless you are requested to do so, don't give illustrations. If you do, one or two will suffice. Remember, you are sowing a delicate seed into the mind of the one you love—give it time to germinate.

8. *Pray about it.* Another big asset for Christians is prayer. Not only is it beneficial in getting us to humble ourselves as we get down on our knees before God, but it realistically brings a third party into our relationship. There is no question that families which pray about their problems and differences have much less heat in dealing with them, because they have someone else vitally involved. When a couple reaches an impasse, both can agree to pray and ask God to help them discern who is right or what course of action should be followed. If they have hurt or insulted one another, after prayer it is a simple thing to apologize and ask forgiveness.

Many communication sessions end with the necessity for one to apologize for violating or not respecting the rights of the other. Next to the three golden words of marriage—"I love you"—is the next most important triplet—"I am sorry." Confession to God eases confession to man.

In this connection it is amazing to me that so many of the Christian couples who believe in prayer (and believe that all Christian couples ought to pray), often neglect to do so. I once took a survey and found that less than 30 percent prayed three times a week. Every Christian couple should pray regularly.

This book will be read by many an individual whose partner is not a Christian or who is so carnal as to refuse to pray. Don't force it. You are not alone; you can "pray to your Father in secret who will reward you openly" (*see* Matthew 6:6). In fact, once you have communicated a matter to your partner, you have through prayer a court of higher appeals to which you can turn. This does two things: it realistically incurs the blessing of God on your problem and it helps you to "back off" once you have stated the issue. This allows your partner to think over your statement. Men are particularly reluctant to admit error, although when filled with the Spirit they do. It is a wise partner who does not demand verbal agreement, since it is a change of behavior you really desire. By prayer you can in faith anticipate such a change, but it must be instituted by God, not you.

9. Commit the matter to God. Once you have communicated on some difficult subject—be it sex, children, finances, mother-in-law, vacation, or the million other problem areas which a marriage and family produces—commit it to God. *Don't nag!* That usually means discuss it only once. Sometimes you may get by with bringing the same subject up a second time, but it is almost always considered nagging to approach it three times. Because all of us are impatient by nature (some temperaments more than others), it is often difficult to wait for the desired change of behavior we seek. This is again another reason that Christian family living is so much to be preferred over an ungodly home. We have a Heavenly Father to whom we can commit our ways, desires, and needs. Of this you can be certain: God blesses those who commit themselves and their problems to Him.

Due to the fact we have addressed the areas where people are hurting in their family life in our several books, Bev and I receive an enormous amount of mail. We have now established a new mail ministry, a division of Family Life Seminars. (For a personal answer to family-life problems not covered in this book, you may write to us at Counseling By Mail, P.O. Box 1299, El Cajon, California 92021.)

We have several examples of God's miraculous response to the Christian who commits his problem to Him, once having made it known to his partner—none more humorous than the lady who wrote to tell us how God worked out a sexual difficulty. The couple had been married eleven years, and although she loved her husband, she had never experienced an orgasm. Like many other women in this modern age when wives know of this possibility, she felt she was being cheated in this area. At a local Christian bookstore she bought *The Act of Marriage*, read it, and suggested her husband do so but to no avail. She then tactfully precipitated a communication session and clearly informed him that she was "unfulfilled" in this area. Her Phlegmatic mate crashed into his shell of self-protection by telling her that "nice girls aren't interested in such things" (as if a man is qualified to know what "nice girls" do in marriage). His wife implored him that the book says that no couple need settle for anything less than mutual satisfaction and again asked him to read it, but he refused.

Recognizing that if she brought it up again, it would be nagging—and seeking to be a woman of God—she prayed about it and committed it to Him. Her letter told us what happened. Her husband was invited to a men's luncheon in a midwestern city where I spoke to a group of men and concluded with a question-and-answer period. A man asked the rather hostile question, "Pastor LaHaye, why did you, a minister, write such a book as *The Act of Marriage?*" It got deathly quiet for a moment so I replied, "For these reasons—first, too many Christian wives have the misconception that lovemaking is evil or ugly. I felt it was time they heard a minister give the biblical perspective that God meant it to be good and beautiful. And second, too many Christian men are so uninformed on the subject that they are cheating their wife and themselves out of a lifetime of happiness." The writer then went on to report that her husband came home from work that evening and rather sheepishly asked, "Where is that marriage book you asked me to read?" He read it, and in a matter of days their love life was transformed. William Cowper said, "God moves in mysterious ways, His wonders to perform."

Knowing and Accepting

There is no subject a married couple should be unable to discuss *sometime*. It should always be done lovingly and honestly, then committed to God and the partner for whatever change is required. Ignoring difficult subjects or problem areas solves nothing and compounds the problem.

Dr. Howard Hendricks has sagely said, "A happy marriage requires two elements: (1) two people who know each other thoroughly [that involves more than knowing a person sexually, although that is included]; and (2) two people who accept each other completely." It is likely that no young couple meets those two qualifications completely, for it takes several years of living with a person and hundreds of hours of communication to know your partner thoroughly and to be so Spirit-controlled that you love and accept each other completely. When you do, you have the ideal relationship. (For a more complete presentation, consult Dr. Dwight Small's excellent book *After You've Said I Do.*)

8

Finances and the Home

The love of money may be the root of all evil, but the *misuse* of money is the beginning of many of life's problems. This can be true for single as well as married people. The fast-talking, high-pressure salesman sooner or later reaches inside the home of every American family.

One college girl called long distance from her dorm to tell her parents about the wonderful opportunity that had just been offered. A company that has had a history of entrapping young women with an "outstanding offer at a reduced student interest rate," had just swept across her campus. She had fallen for their high-pitched sales talk and believed she could not be happy without their merchandise. She excitedly told about paying "only one dollar a week for six months, then two dollars a week for two years, and twenty-five dollars a month after graduation—until it was paid off" (which seemed to be rather an indefinite period). After the interest rate was added, plus the years of payments, it figured out that she was being charged double the price. Her parents finally concluded that if this taught her a valuable lifetime lesson about credit, then it would be worth the extra money she would have to pay. Like so many other

178

"buy now—pay later" contracts, the payments would still be going on long after the thrill and worth of the purchases were over. If she had been forced to pay cash, there would have been no question about her ability to purchase the item, but when she was told that the payments would only be "one or two dollars per week," she concluded that was certainly within her reach.

This type of advertising and buying propaganda causes much of the turmoil in American homes today. Buying on credit encourages people to make purchases they cannot afford and perhaps do not need. It has put a new emphasis on possession of material things that is unhealthy and produces an indifferent attitude toward the cost of purchases made. The "good life" is represented to young couples as a quick accumulation on credit, of a houseful of furniture and other possessions that would normally take ten to fifteen years of marriage. So many couples within the first few years have surrounded and encumbered their lives with credit from all directions. This "buying power" does not stop while they catch up, but like a contagious disease it creeps on—month after month.

The basic problem in over 70 percent of the marriages that fail stems from finances. When you compound the normal conflicts and disagreements in a home with the financial pressures from overspending and credit-buying, the end results can be hostility, bitterness, and in severe cases, divorce. The insidious enemy in many of these marriages has undoubtedly been credit and the you-can't-live-without-them credit cards. In the earliest stages of marriage, couples rush out to apply for credit so they can become established, only to find later on that credit was their worst enemy and that whatever they had established was now beginning to crumble. Credit-buying encourages "impulse" purchasing, giving extra lavish gifts, plus excessive spending—simply because you can take home the merchandise without laying down the cash. Finally, the day of reckoning comes—when all the charge slips are totalled, and the end-of-the-month statements begin to roll in. Tension mounts, irritability sets in, and tempers flare. What started out to be a normal way of living suddenly turns into a hotbed of frustration and accusations.

How Financial Pressures Reveal Themselves

1. Excessive shopping.   Financial pressures bring on a depressed spirit, and some experience a temporary relief from depression by purchasing more new items. Of course, in the end, this only compounds the already existing problem.

2. Critical spirit.   A woman is especially guilty of this when under pressure. She will begin to pick and nag about everything the husband does that not quite suits her, even to the point of blowing small things out of proportion. This gives her an escape valve to let off some of the inner pressure that has been building up.

3. Lying and deceit.   The most common and complex way to hide money matters is by lying. Both husbands and wives are guilty of financial deceit in order to satisfy their material impulses. When money is spent lavishly or foolishly, they discover the need to lie in order to get out of a difficult financial situation and their own embarrassment.

4. Seeking self-pity.   This person talks about the financial problems over and over again, in the hopes that others will feel sorry for him and provide a temporary comfort. If there is no obvious effort for self-help, sympathy will do more harm than good.

5. Extreme fatigue.   It may come on very slowly, until they cannot remember when they began to feel so tired. Living with irritation and accusations causes one to feel defeated before he ever begins.

6. Psychological illnesses. Tensions and stress over a long period of time are the greatest contributors toward self-induced illnesses. Anyone living under the pressure of "final notices" or collectors' calls is certainly a ripe candidate for this problem.

7. Angry accusations. Accusations of stupidity, indifference, in-law interference, and selfishness are a few of the darts that are thrown back and forth. It is easier to blame the other partner for the financial mess in the family than to accept much of the problem as one's own and set forth to correct it.

8. Temporary frigidity. It is very difficult to continue a close sexual relationship when tension is mounting and resentments are building. If this condition continues for a long period of time, the temporary frigidity can grow and develop into a sexual hopelessness for that marriage. One husband said that he felt as if he were paying to have intercourse with his wife—she only engaged in lovemaking when the money flowed freely.

9. Silent treatment. When the sexual relationship comes to a halt, it is not long before communication ceases, at least *normal* communication. There may be screaming and yelling from one side, while the other partner clams up and remains silent. The silent one is usually filled with resentment toward the other partner. The more one is silent, the more the other screams, until conditions move from bad to worse.

10. Finally, separation. In the midst of despair, many couples falsely believe that they can better work out their problems if they separate. At this point in the marriage, most couples are not able to think too soundly and therefore are willing to escape reality and run from the financial mess they are in. Before couples reach this point, they should follow the wise advice given in Proverbs 12:15: "The way of a fool is right in his own eyes, But a wise man is he who listens to counsel" (NAS).

It seems that the money problem in marriage relationships is the last one about which a couple will seek counsel. When couples face sexual difficulties, turmoil with children, and so on, they are more willing to find help than when they face financial disaster. Men especially feel that this is a reflection on their male superiority, and ego keeps them from seeking help. Too often they wait until it is too late and the damage has already been done. The Bible says that a wise man is one who takes heed of counsel.

Money Is in God's Plan

Money is necessary and a part of God's plan for His people. It is only the love of money and its misuse that are destructive. The Bible has much instruction for us on how to manage our money. Therefore, we must conclude that how we handle it is a part of our Christian walk.

I recommend that a young couple (or any couple for that matter) talk over and develop a single budget, so both husband and wife are well aware of where their money is going. Many couples have found this to be a real eye-opener and a tremendous help in solving the money pressures they have created (or even before they are created). The main purpose of a budget is to identify and put controls on the excessive and miscellaneous spending. Don't scoff at a budget! If you are already in debt, then you desperately need one to help you balance your spending with your income. Proverbs 16:9 NAS: "The mind of man plans his way, But the Lord directs his steps." The first step of planning is a simple, useful budget.

You cannot plan a budget and expect God to direct your steps, until you are willing to honor Him with the firstfruits of your income. In other words, obey God and plan your tithe the very first thing. " 'Bring the whole tithe into the storehouse, so that there may be food in My house, and test Me now in this,' says the Lord of hosts, 'if I will not open for you the windows of heaven, and pour out for you a blessing until there is no more need' " (Malachi 3:10 NAS). Now *there* is a promise that you cannot afford to pass up. The Lord says to test Him by giving the whole tithe to Him—and He will bless you until there is no more need. It sounds impossible, but remember that our God deals in the impossible things of life and He challenges you to test Him.

During our first year of marriage, we were both students in college—and money was very tight. Tim was a GI and his tuition was covered by veterans' benefits. The amount allotted us for living expenses was $120 per month, which had to cover tithe, rent, food, transportation, clothing, and my college tuition. There was no way it could stretch that far, and we consistently ran behind. We also pastored a little country church thirty-five miles away on weekends. This offered fifteen dollars a week, barely enough to cover the travel expenses. We were very happy in our first church and trusted God to work out our impossible financial situation. At one point my college tuition was due, and we did not have the money to cover it. In fact, between us we had fifty cents to last two weeks. Again we trusted God to help us through the next two weeks by stretching that fifty cents—and we committed my tuition bill to Him. The next day Tim went to our mailbox and found a check to cover my tuition exactly. Various states paid veterans a "bonus" and the state of Michigan was the first to pay this. During those days we tithed very scrupulously every bit of income we received. God "passed the test," as far as we were concerned.

Several years ago, Tim challenged the members of our congregation to step out by faith and raise their tithe for the year to 20 percent. It was called "double tithing" and was a real act of faith for the many families who committed themselves to this increased giving. At the close of the year, we spoke with many families to see if any had continued this 20-percent giving for the entire year. Out hearts were thrilled as we heard family after family testify of God's great faithfulness to them. Over and over we heard stories about how God had stretched their 80 percent further than they could have stretched the full 100 percent. Not one of these families experienced financial hardship for that year. We should not have been surprised, because—after all— that is exactly what He promised to do. But even now as I record this story on paper, my heart is filled to overflowing when I think that God in His great faithfulness will never disappoint us when He makes a promise to us.

This experience occurred during one of the most serious recessions we have had in our city, and unemployment was extremely high. While attending a ministers' meeting, Tim heard a local pastor comment on how many men in his congregation were out of work, so he inquired as to the size of his congregation. When he returned to the office, he counted the number of our own members who were unemployed and, comparing the size of our congregation with theirs, found that our unemployment level was eighteen times lower than theirs. Several men reported during those days that others in their departments were laid off during serious cutbacks, but for some "mysterious" reason our men seemed to be supernaturally protected. You cannot outgive the Lord!

The minimum tithe is usually considered to be 10 percent. However, the Old Testament required 23⅓ percent—and if a man gave less, he was robbing God. Each couple must determine what percentage to give, keeping in mind the biblical principle: ". . . he who sows sparingly shall also reap sparingly; and he who sows bountifully shall also reap bountifully. Let each one do just as he purposed in his heart; not grudgingly or under compulsion; for God loves a cheerful giver" (2 Corinthians 9:6, 7 NAS).

Mortgage Payments

In today's inflationary economy, it is utterly impossible for a young couple to own a house and car without mortgage payments. The safeguard for purchasing a car would be to make sure that the down payment is high enough so that the amount owed is not greater than the resale value of the car. Don't be bitten by the "car bug" that makes you discontent with an older car. Last year, as we traveled in 42 foreign countries, we found many American-made cars being driven with well over 300,000 (and even 400,000) miles on them. In America we have been led to believe that after 100,000 miles there isn't much good left in a car. Precaution should be taken not to attempt buying a home and a new car in the same year. This could be financial suicide. When you take on a mortage, either for a home or a car, the debt begins on the date the monthly payment is due. Be certain that the payments are low enough so that you can pay them as scheduled. Before going into debt for a house or car, carefully examine your other expenditures to be sure they are trimmed down to enable you to take on another monthly payment.

We are instructed in Psalms: "The wicked borrows and does not pay back, But the righteous is gracious and gives" (37:21 NAS). Proverbs 22:7 states: "The rich rules over the poor, And the borrower becomes the lender's slave" (NAS). It reminds us very strongly that God wants us to have financial freedom regardless of what our income might be.

To enable you to trim down any excessive spending, here are a few basic questions that should be asked before each purchase that is not considered an absolute necessity for survival:

1. Do we need the item?
2. Do we have the money to pay cash (or not exceeding our credit capability)?
3. Is it high on our priority list?
4. Did we pray about it?
5. Have we shopped for the best buy?

If all these questions can be answered with a positive, then ask one more—

6. Did we ask God to either confirm or remove the desire for it?

If still *yes,* then proceed wisely. If answers are negative, then thank God for keeping you from making an unwise purchase.

Planning a Budget

There are many books available to help couples plan a simple and workable budget. George M. Bowman has shared a guide to budget planning in his book *Here's How to Succeed With Your Money.* He suggests that, after tithe and taxes are paid, the balance of income should be divided by the 10-70-20 plan.

10%	Savings and Investments
70%	Living Expenses
20%	Debts and Buffer Fund

I would like to break it down further and offer the following percentages for a family of four whose total income would be between $15,000 and $20,000 annually. For this example, we will use the middle figure of approximately $17,500 annual salary (family of four). All amounts are rounded to the nearest dollar.

Expenses Off the Top	% of Total	Annual Outlay	Monthly Outlay
Tithe	10	$1,750	$146
Taxes	14	2,450	204
Total	24	4,200	$350

The balance (76% of the total $17,500) will be divided into percentages totalling 100% of this $13,300.

Expenses	%	Annual	Monthly
Housing (payments, taxes, insurance, utilities)	32	$4,256	$354
Automobile (payments, gas, oil, repairs, insurance, license)	14	1,862	155
Food (not junk food!)	24	3,192	266
Insurance (life, health, disability)	6	798	67
Clothing (Shop wisely.)	7	931	78
Debts (This is the item most needing careful surveillance.)	6	798	67
Miscellaneous (entertainment, recreation, vacation)	6	798	67
Medical, dental, prescriptions (This is assuming average health and that you have group medical insurance.)	5	665	55
Savings (If you have had a good year, without many medical bills, auto repairs, and so on, use any excess for a savings account. This will enable you to be a cash buyer and eventually eliminate the 6% for debts. The purpose of this is to help you rid yourself of the credit cards.)	?	?	?
Total	100	$13,300	$1,109

The above is just a suggested shell of a budget. It will not work *for* you—you must work at it. If you have been deeply in debt, do not expect a budget to solve your problems overnight. It will take much sacrifice and self-denial to put your financial house in order. But remember—it can be done. The peace of mind and the order that is restored to your home will be well worth all the denials and limits you put on your spending.

Who Should Handle the Money?

This question should be openly discussed before the marriage begins, so each one knows how the other feels about the subject. There is no absolute answer to this question. However, after counseling many couples in the midst of their conflicts, we have come to believe that it is important in the first few years of married life that the husband handles the finances. During this time, the new bride should be adjusting to a spirit of submission and teamwork. If she is handling the money, this is one area in which she does not have to learn to submit—because she is in control. Usually it can be said that the one who handles the money controls the family, particularly in the first few years.

After the wife has adjusted to her new husband's role as head of the house, if they are both in full agreement, she could take over the family bookkeeping. Even then, it must be a team effort. The family income belongs to both of them, and together they should plan and agree on how it should be spent. There should be no money secrets between them if they are going to have harmony in their marriage.

Each partner should be allowed an equal amount of money to be used as personal spending money. The amount is not the important factor. A person can adjust to varying amounts. It may be used for gifts for others or for one's own personal needs. The important thing is that it is a fund, however small, that is used any way one chooses, In the suggested budget on the previous page, it would come under the item of "miscellaneous."

Some couples have agreed on splitting the responsibility of bookkeeping. The husband deposits the paycheck in his account and then writes a check to his wife to deposit in her checkbook. Here would be the budgeted amount for food, clothing for family, sundries, and her own personal fund. The husband keeps in his checkbook the balance to cover tithe, taxes, house and auto payments, insurance, debts, and so on, plus his own personal fund that is equal to his wife's.

It is important for the husband to keep in mind that a woman does not like to ask for every dollar she receives. Too often a husband will hold such a tight grip on his wallet that it has created a spirit of bitterness and resentment in his wife. Finally, in exasperation, she explodes—and he wonders, "What in the world is wrong with her?" She spends an equal time keeping the family together and the household functioning well. Does she not deserve an equal say in how the money should be handled?

Working Wives

This heading may be misleading because it implies that some wives work and others do not. Every wife that is worth anything will be a "working" wife. However, some will work in the home, others outside, and there will be those who must do both, at least for a while.

In today's economy, most young wives find it advantageous to work for a year or two before they start a family. In many cases it becomes necessary in order for a young couple to handle the high cost of rent, food, and transportation. However, it is wise for couples to adjust as quickly as possible to living on only the husband's income. The wife's salary should be "extra" money that is allowed to accumulate for a down payment on a home, or perhaps used to pay off college debts. Whatever the "extra" may be, care should be taken not to depend on the second income for living expenses. Unfortunately, all too often, the couple enjoys the luxury of two incomes and may postpone buying a home and starting a family. It is at this strategic time that some couples decide that having a family is too costly so they head toward a childless future.

If the wife continues to work after the children come, there are more complications to face. There will be the need for baby-sitters who will spend more time with the children during their waking hours than the mother will. Likewise, the mother will spend the best hours of her day—when she is most alert, patient, kind, responsive, and ambitious— away from her children. The couple needs to analyze the wife's wages against the additional expenses that working generates. In addition, both need to consider the federal, state, and social-security taxes, plus tithe. Some of the common expenses that must come out of the remainder would be baby-sitting fees, additional meals in restaurants, noneconomical fast meals at home, transportation to and from work, parking fees, increased wardrobe, and perhaps extra help in the home.

It might prove to be better economically if the wife stayed at home, saved on baby-sitting fees, planned delicious low-cost, home-cooked meals, plus cut the additional expenses and considered a part-time job that she could do at home. I have discovered several ways that women can earn extra money at home and I am sure there are many more. A few such jobs would be typing labels, stuffing envelopes, baby-sitting for someone else, teaching piano lessons if qualified, typing term papers for local college students, typing manuscripts, or doing neighborhood sewing. When their children enter school, some women have been able to find employment where the hours of work coincided with the school hours. This allows them to be home when the children arrive. The creative woman will find a way to make the budget stretch and still be able to spend time to raise her own children. I feel that it is extremely important for a mother not to work away from home while she still has preschool children. These first few years of life are the most important, and no one is going to be as concerned and diligent in the children's training as their own mother.

There are more and more parents who feel the urgent need to give their elementary and high-school children a Christian education. It does cost additional money which may not be in the budget. In some cases mothers whose children are in school may consider getting a job during those hours to pay the cost of a Christian education. Because of the moral and philosophical problems caused by many public schools, a Christian education is gaining an increasingly higher priority with many Christian parents.

May I suggest that the Christian community be careful to examine the financial arrangements of their pastors and families. In years past, ministers have been underpaid, and many wives were forced to go to work just to keep body and soul together. As Christian women saw the wife of the pastor going outside the home to work, they followed her example—and it was not always an absolute necessity for them. Consequently, we have many Christian families today in which the children have been and are being raised by baby-sitters.

We must recognize that there are situations today where mothers have no choice but to work outside the home.

There may have been a death of the husband, divorce, or separation. What a wonderful chance this is for another mother, who may need to work herself, to become a substitute mother (or baby-sitter) to help raise these children in love and good training. Both families can benefit from such an act of Christian grace as this.

Another danger for working wives must be mentioned. When a wife gets a job working outside the home for an employer, she has to meet certain qualifications. For example, she must be neat and attractive; she submits to the employer's authority while at the office; she is polite and appreciative, alert and productive, flexible in maintaining a work schedule in keeping with the employer's plans. These are all examples of a businesswoman, but are also good characteristics of an ideal wife. It is possible for these interests and concerns to be confused and compared to the partner at home. The feeling can develop that the "partner" at the office is more efficient and capable than the one at home, and this is when danger sets in.

A Christian Should Have a Will

Good stewardship involves making a will that not only provides for your loved ones, but also designates a percentage or a tithe of your estate to be given to a Christian organization of your choice. What a lasting testimony it can be when, after your death, your money continues on in the Lord's work. We are closely involved with the Development Department of Christian Heritage College in San Diego. Since Tim was one of the founders of the college, we do take a keen interest in its continuing development. The head of this department has told us on several occasions that when he is called in for consultation regarding a will, he always suggests that the parties leave a tithe of their estate to Christian work. It is interesting that many times this comes as a total surprise to people who had never considered it before. These people were all Christians and no doubt good stewards of their money while living. But the thrill comes in knowing that, even after your death, you can be faithful in distributing your money as the Bible instructs.

If a person dies without a will, the state will dispose of the property according to the state law, and that could impose hardships and restrictions on the family left behind. Consult with a lawyer who can write the will for you at a reasonable fee. The day will surely come when it will be worth all the planning devoted to disposing of your earthly possessions.

Last year, before we left on our nine-month around-the-world missionary trip, we were advised to update our will. Now that was a startling thought at first, because we had every intention of returning home. But we followed this good advice and met with our lawyer to finalize the papers. Just a few days before we left the country, we called our four children and the two married partners to our home for the evening. It was our plan to share with them what we had done and to inform them of the percentages we requested be left to specific Christian organizations. We did not want it to be a surprise to them. It was a time of heavy serious talk and then we had prayer together. What a joy it was to let them in on our burden for these organizations and hear them share it also as they joined us in prayer for each one. That will was accomplishing much in the lives of our own children even before our death.

An important part of the Christian life is the discipline of keeping one's financial house in proper order. "Let all things be done decently and in order" (1 Corinthians 14:40).

9

The Church and Your Family

On a scale of one to eight, where your family decides to go to church will rank about number five in life's most important decisions. The first four cover accepting Christ as your Lord and Saviour, deciding on a vocation, selecting a partner, and choosing a place to live. Unfortunately, most Christians do not realize the great influence of the church on their family.

Of the three institutions founded by God Himself (family, civil government, and church), only the church is supportive of the family. Active participation in a Bible-teaching church will provide many safeguards against the erosion of family life. The church is the best agency for training people in the principles of happy family living. Consequently, the church enjoys a much lower divorce level than that of the secular community. Of the 890 active families in our church, which is probably typical of Bible-teaching churches for Southern California, there are 40 which have been struck by divorce. In other words, one out of twenty-two families have experienced divorce—compared to one out of two in the community in general.

This means that Christian marriages are eleven times as stable as nonchurch unions. If the divorce rate is lowered eleven times, we can assume that the happiness quotient is increased equally. (Southern California churches may have a higher rate of divorce than Christians nationally, because many divorced believers move west after undergoing such a trauma—thus inflating these numbers.) However, the divorce rate has also increased alarmingly in churches throughout America, because many Christians imitate the world and its ways rather than obediently following the principles of God.

A couple who visited our Sunday-morning service introduced themselves and said, "Before buying a lot and building a house, we wanted to be sure there was a good church in this community." I wish more Christians demonstrated such foresight. Most folks who built in that area probably had no idea what kind of church was available. Since ours was the only one for several miles, it could have been tragic for them and their children if we had not preached the Gospel.

Some Christians do not understand that the church they attend can be a dynamic influence on their entire family. It can help them mature spiritually, enrich their marriage relationship, and enable their children to face life's adjustments. Or it can freeze them spiritually and seriously jeopardize every area of their lives. A Bible-teaching church with a life-related message can make it considerably easier for parents to discharge their responsibilities to raise their children in the fear and admonition of the Lord.

Wherever the Gospel has been preached, churches have sprung up. In New Testament times it was customary for Christians to meet in homes or halls on a regular basis for the study of the Bible, fellowship with one another, and the "breaking of bread." Such meetings helped new Christians to grow in the faith, to face persecution, and to go out and share their faith in the power of the Holy Spirit.

Through nineteen centuries of history, bodies of believers have regularly joined together. These assemblies, or churches, have been the instruments by which God has kept His message alive and presented it to the world. Satan has consistently tried to destroy them through persecution, heresy, division, apostasy, friction, worldly conformity, and a host of other vicious or subtle attacks.

In the course of the centuries, God has raised up certain groups and organizations which have been mightily used in such specialized areas as youth, missions, education, and so on. Some of them have hit a peak in effectiveness and then faded away. The one tool God has used through the centuries—and is still using—is His church.

The last book of the Bible describes seven local churches as "lampstands" (or lighthouses) of the Gospel (Revelation 1–3). It pictures Christ walking among the lampstands, or churches, willing to empower, enlighten, and provide for any church that wants to do His will. This great book of prophecy indicates that our Lord ordained the continuing ministry of the local church. In the Gospel of Matthew, He said of the church, ". . . the gates of hell shall not prevail against it" (Matthew 16:18). The church is the only permanent institution the family can still rely on.

Today the local church is one of the few places where the spiritual life of an individual can be nurtured. Television, radio, magazines, newspapers, all other news media, and the public schools are practically devoid of any contribution to spiritual edification. Instead, they propagate philosophies that are worldly and quite contrary to the Word of God.

There was a time when the principles of the Bible were applied in most aspects of life. Our economy was based on integrity and hard work. Many laws were based on scriptural teaching. Every man was responsible for himself, but biblical concern for one's neighbor was a way of life. Christian principles were not always practiced, but basically they were the accepted standards. Our schools recognized the existence of God and used the Bible freely in the classroom.

Today all that has been changed. Parents who want their children to learn the truth about God can expect little or no help from the schools. The best place to expose them to Christian teaching—next to the home itself—is the church. Through its Bible-teaching services, Sunday school, youth groups, Bible studies, and other activities, the church is equipped to contribute to the spiritual training of the whole family. Apart from Christian periodicals and books, if a person neglects the church, his family is almost certain to grow up with an entirely secular education and philosophy of life.

The church is probably the most underrated organization in the world today. Admittedly, it is not perfect—but it is the tool created especially by God to reach the world for Christ. The church is indispensable to a Christian and his family.

Purpose of the Church

If it teaches the Bible, a church can fulfill a unique position, by offering something vital to every member of a family. The Scriptures were written to help spiritual "children . . . young men . . . and fathers" (1 John 2:12–14). When the Bible is properly taught, it provides spiritual food for every person, adapted to his personal needs.

A church also meets the basic need of every human being to serve his fellowman. As we shall see, anyone who sincerely wants to help another may do so in his local church—in teaching, youth work, visitation, or whatever he is qualified to do. A church also provides opportunities for enjoyable fellowship and making friends on every level. At church, wholesome relationships can be formed. Children, young people, newlyweds, parents, and senior citizens are going to make friends somewhere—where better than in the church, where they are likely to find people of similar interests and standards?

How to Choose a Church

Since one's church can have such a profound effect on your life, the selection of a church is vitally important. One should not just attend the nearest church. The first consideration is usually the denomination—but the final decision should be based on the message preached and the opportunity for biblical worship and service, as well as on the total potential impact on the entire family.

The following suggestions will be helpful in choosing a family church:

1. Pray for wisdom. God promises wisdom (James 1:5) for those who seek His counsel in making decisions. The entire family should join in this prayer, for the chosen church will be everyone's spiritual home. Good human judgment is important, but only God knows what a church will be two, five, or twenty years from now.

2. Loyalty to the Bible is a primary characteristic of a good church. As you visit various churches, evaluate them in the light of how much balanced and careful exposure to the Word of God your family will receive there. Examine the Sunday-school literature for Bible content. No amount of enthusiasm, promotion, or organization can replace solid Bible teaching.

Church services vary, depending on the denomination and the area of the country. Your tastes and preferences are more than likely based on your background and temperament. Churches, like people, have personalities. It is important to feel comfortable in your home church, but comfort or enjoyment of form is not as important as Bible teaching. It is possible to go sound asleep in a "comfortable" church and, before you realize it, start drifting spiritually.

My uncle, Dr. Elmer Palmer, was a pastor for fifty-three years. When I was twenty-five and just starting out in the ministry, he advised me, "Feed the people big hunks of beefsteak from the Word of God every time you preach." As a result I have always given my sermons "The Beefsteak Test." That is, do they contain a great deal of Bible and a little of Tim LaHaye? That kind of preaching builds strong spiritual members, so look for that type of church for your family.

3. Your church should minister to your entire family. Some churches are strong in youth work, some in the area of children, and some provide a fine program for adults. Visit the youth meetings, Sunday school, or training-hour departments which members of your family will attend, so you will know firsthand what is being taught and who is teaching it. If you want your children and young people to remain open to the leading of the Holy Spirit for a lifetime of Christian service, examine your prospective church to see how many of its former youth are in or preparing for Christian work. It is estimated that over 85 percent of today's pastors and missionaries responded to God's call to service in Sunday school, church, or youth camp.

Many good churches are catching the vision of starting

Christian schools. The deterioration of the public schools morally, spiritually, philosophically—and (according to recently published test scores) educationally—causes Christian parents to look to their church for the proper education of their children. In an increasing number of public schools, the incidence of violence, rape, and drug abuse renders them totally unacceptable to the Christian community. Personally, I am convinced, after fifteen years of involvement in Christian-school education, that it is the wave of the future. I am praying that so many churches and Christians will become concerned about the problem that by 1990, 51 percent of all educable children in America will be attending Christian schools. Lest you think I am exaggerating, let me tell you this story . . . . While being evaluated for accreditation (which we subsequently received) by the Western Association of Schools and Colleges, our high school was visited by a team of five educators. One was a Christian who quickly identified himself. Three were principals of enormous public high schools in their respective communities. Two of them confidentially shared with me that they sent their daughters to *Christian* schools in their community. A week or so later I attended a social activity and met the president of the San Diego Unified School Board, who told me his daughter attended our Christian high school and loved it.

4. Your church should provide you a place to serve God. Admittedly, there may be other areas of Christian service in your community, but usually a Christian can work most effectively in his own church. Most churches require that you be a member before you teach or hold an office. The pastor, Christian-education director, or Sunday-school superintendent will tell you if your prospective church needs your services.

5. Your church should be one you can confidently recommend to others. Every Christian should anticipate that God will use him as a witness—at his work, in his neighborhood, or in his other contacts. It is not enough for you to lead people to Christ—your new converts will need Christian fellowship and Bible instruction in a warmly spiritual environment. It is easier to get them to meet you at your church than send them to another church alone.

Get the Most From Your Church

Once you have settled on the church you feel God is leading you to, join it. Make it your family's spiritual home. One of the oldest clichés reminds us, "You get out of a thing only what you put into it." Some Christians sow so little seed that they harvest next to nothing.

Most churches expect their members to assume some responsibilities—as much for the members' good as for the benefit of the church. You and your family will receive rich blessings when you faithfully fulfill such responsibilities.

Every church has a few members who attend every service; they usually reap the greatest dividends. Others attend both Sunday morning and evening but never come to week-night services. The majority gain minimum blessing from their church because they attend only on Sunday morning. The more secular our society becomes, the more believers need to expose themselves to the Word of God—an experience which most Christians enjoy only at the services of their churches.

There are 168 hours in a week. Obviously, one or two hours spent in the Lord's house, studying His Word, is meager compared to the time devoted to life's other activities. Though the Word of God is the most important subject of study for a Christian, most believers do not give

it as much time as they devote to the daily newspaper.
One common hindrance to regular family church attendance is the notion that we may embitter teenagers by forcing them to go to church. On a number of occasions through
the years, I have heard overindulgent parents say, "I don't
make my child go to church. He might grow up to hate it."
One Christian couple told their son that if he didn't want
to attend church, he could go to the local drugstore and get
a malted while waiting for his parents. Somehow my sermons never seemed to compete with that lad's love for
malteds, and today—married and the father of three—he
still does not attend church.

In that same church was a family with five sons. Their
father made the decision for them: Every Sunday they went
to church. They sat with their parents during morning worship but were permitted to sit with friends at other services,
if their conduct warranted such liberty. Today one boy is on
the mission field and the others are active leaders in local
churches.

Don't be afraid of making the decision for your young
people about attending church. You don't hesitate to send
them to school, whether they want to go or not. And how
often do your children *want* to visit the dentist or the doctor? But you make them go if they *need* to. Your children
desperately need the church and the consistent opportunity
it gives them to worship and to learn God's will. I thank
God for my mother who, when I was a rebellious
seventeen-year-old, made it clear that I was to be at practically every service our church held. I doubt that I would be
in the ministry today if I had been left to make my own
decisions about church attendance during those years!

Forcing a child to attend services doesn't turn him
against the church. It is often hypocrisy in the home that
makes a shallow mockery of the church. I have seen few

children from consistent Christian homes go down the drain. Among the few who have, most come back to their faith later in life (*see* Proverbs 22:6).

Another duty that brings a blessing to church members is the giving of their tithes and offerings. The Lord Jesus said, "For where your treasure is, there will your heart be also" (Matthew 6:21). You will never develop the proper love for and interest in your local church until you invest some of yourself in it. Your church needs your financial support, but you need to learn the joy of giving to the work of the Lord on a regular basis. The Old Testament standard of giving was the tithe, or tenth. The New Testament standard is "as God has prospered you." Shouldn't Christians at least come up to the ancient Jewish standard? When you give your tithes and offerings through your local church, you gain a distinct advantage since it is one of the few Christian organizations that provides its donors with a financial report. You vote on elected trustees who administer the finances and thus are assured a good degree of integrity by people you know and trust.

One of the duties most lightly esteemed by many church members is attendance at business meetings. This may sound insignificant, but you would be amazed how few people care enough about the operation of their own church to participate in its business. Several pastor friends have told me they can hardly muster enough people for a quorum. I would be the first to admit that church business meetings are not the most inspirational sessions to attend, but their importance to the church requires that they be given priority.

For any organization to function, it must have leaders. The only way to limit the number of business meetings a church must hold is to have leaders who can operate the church effectively. Your church has a right to expect you to devote some of your time to its business.

There are other areas in which your church needs you, and the Lord will lead you into them if you are available. One of the finest church laymen I know is an executive in a large industrial manufacturing company. Each year he looks over his church to discover areas of greatest need. He makes himself available to the Lord, his pastor, and the officers in the church. If he is given a job, he dedicates himself to performing well and tries to train another layman to replace him in the future. Sometimes the church isn't ready to delegate the job to his trainee after the first year, so he stays on one year more. Only God knows the full effectiveness of this man's ministry.

No church is perfect! The late Dr. Harry A. Ironside used to say, "If you find the perfect church, don't join it—you'll ruin it!" You are bound to find things wrong with your church. But *never* criticize it, the pastor, the leaders, or the members in front of your children. Many thoughtless words of parental criticism against some detail have turned children against the whole church.

Parents, not the church, are the real losers in a case like this—but so are their children. Instead of criticizing your church, put your shoulder to the wheel and *change* it. And if the wrong is not in an area of your responsibility, commit it to God. After all, it's really *His* church; He is well able to take care of it.

Social Life and Your Church

God has made most of us with a craving for social life. We want to be loved, sought out, and included in whatever is going on. The church has the potential of being one of the finest sources of social contact, but unfortunately the selfish and impersonal attitude of the world is too often carried over into the social life of the church.

Many people are lonely and hungry for fellowship. They visit your church hoping to make friends, but often those to whom they look for friendship do nothing to meet their need. Have you ever opened your home to such people? Many church members never do. They are busy enjoying the friends they already have. It takes a little work—you may have to bake some cookies and put on a pot of coffee—but you'll be amazed how rewarding it is!

Have you ever thought about the social vacuum many new converts are plunged into when they join a church? If they were active social types before their conversion, they are often in for a discouraging experience when they lose interest in some of their worldly activities and look to the church. Too frequently, it is difficult or impossible for these strangers to break into the cliques that have established themselves in a church. We don't like to admit it, but cliques develop all too easily when we naturally gravitate to our friends. Remember that new or prospective Christians need your love and attention far more than your old friends do!

Several years ago, three couples in our church hit on a novel idea. They decided to share in providing dinner in one of their homes for themselves and three other couples once a month. They would invite one regular-member family and two new couples. Within two years they had more friends in the church than anyone else. Their own spiritual growth has been amazing, and today one of these couples serves as missionaries in Ecuador, another joined the staff of Campus Crusade, and the third is counted among the pillars of our church.

One Spirit-filled woman I know decided to volunteer as the social chairman of an adult Sunday-school class. The Bible teaching was good on Sunday, but the class members were impersonal and aloof toward each other. She soon had things jumping—by careful planning and by involving many others who were waiting for someone to invite them to climb down out of the grandstand. Instead of one big social a month, she would often arrange to have eight or ten small groups meeting in various parts of the city. Sometimes she would ask people in a certain geographical area to serve a snack after church and to invite class visitors. Her service as a Sunday-school-class chairman had real impact on the whole Sunday-school's attendance. Sporadic visitors to Sunday school became regular in their attendance, some invited their unsaved friends, and a number received Christ during this woman's two years of service.

Since adults were attending more regularly and bringing their children and young people, the entire Sunday school experienced its largest growth rate in our church's history—and that woman was probably the most important single reason. Lifetime friendships were made in that adult class, and many of them were hers.

Hospitality With a Purpose

Christians should be "given to hospitality." Never have more Christians had nicer homes in which to be hospitable, yet somehow other pursuits too often take priority over entertaining those who need our hospitality.

A young dentist called one day and asked if we would come over on a Sunday evening after church to help him and his wife dedicate their new home. It was packed with church friends when we arrived, and we enjoyed a warm time of singing, prayer, and fellowship. They told the group they wanted God to use their home for His glory, and during the next few years hundreds of people were their guests. Only God knows how many have been drawn to Him by this generous Christian hospitality.

Many Christians in all parts of the country are using their homes in hospitality-evangelism. Some have informal Bible studies and refreshments; others have tapes or speakers. Their experience shows that many are hungry for the Word of God. Home Bible studies provide a neutral place for new converts to bring unsaved friends to study the Word. At first these "prospects" may not be willing to go to a church, but usually they aren't reluctant to attend a Bible study in a hospitable Christian home.

One couple has led more people to Christ and into our church than any other that I know of, and they have used their home to do it. About three years after their conversion, they started to entertain their unsaved friends and some of their new Christian friends from the church. One night they stumbled on the idea of playing a taped sermon and then discussing it over coffee and dessert. Now the couple listens to the tape in advance, thinks up questions to spark discussion, and then invites twenty or thirty people, aiming at a balance of one unsaved person to two Christians. Since neither of them has had any formal Bible training, they try to make sure there are two or three mature believers among their guests.

Through the years I have seen these folks lead doctors, dentists, lawyers, plumbers, mechanics, and housewives to faith in Christ. One refreshing aspect of their work is that they do not concentrate on the "up-and-outer." To them the couple with the rickety old car is as important as the owner of the luxury sedan. After watching them, I am convinced that their ministry could be duplicated by any Christian willing to make his home available to God.

"Hospitality with a purpose" is a form of Christian service that has its origin in the church, is based on the home, and is pointed toward reaching people. Christians often think their home is not good enough to entertain in, but other people aren't primarily interested in your furnishings or in the refreshments you serve. They will love you for including them as your guests. That's why this kind of ministry can be so effective—because of the need for love and acceptance. More people are won to Christ through love than through logic.

If you are interested in using your home for "hospitality with a purpose," offer it to God in prayer and start experimenting with some of these suggestions or others the Lord may give you. It won't be long before you'll feel comfortable in a ministry of hospitality.

How Best to Serve

The church is one of the best employment opportunities in the world, for it is a place where everyone may—and should—serve. Any dedicated Christian who wants to be used by God can find something to do in the Sunday school, the nursery, the youth programs, or driving a bus, visiting, having home Bible classes, and so on.

There is tremendous therapy in Christian service. Every human being needs to invest himself in something for the good of his fellowman. Nothing equals the significance of Christian service, for through it you not only help a person live a better life but enable him to face eternity.

Practically everyone today is concerned about the problems of young people—rebellion, dope, sex, and many other areas. But few people are willing to do much about the situation. The same is true in the church—everyone wants a dynamic youth ministry, but it is harder to attract youth sponsors for such a ministry than to get almost any other workers in the church. People have the false notion that one must possess special talent or training to work with young people. Really, today's young people aren't that "different." The primary requirement for a Christian who is to work with children or youth is love for them. Even the hardest cases respond to patient, tactful Christian love.

The best way to learn how to work with young people is by doing it. Good books, seminars, and clinics are available to help you master techniques—but experience and necessity are still excellent teachers. We have found that parents with young people of their own in a given department make great helpers in a youth group for that age. Their children, rather than feeling uncomfortable in such a setup, are usually pleased to have their parents that much involved.

Most young people, sooner or later, go through an uncooperative phase and decide, "I'm not going." If the parent gives in, he is making a big mistake. If young people don't attend youth meetings and socials, they soon drift out into the world and make friends that take them away from the church. It seems better to insist, if necessary, that your teens go to youth activities and take their unsaved friends with them from time to time. Many a Christian today was an unsaved teenager whose buddy took him to church youth functions.

By our own example, we need to teach our children and youth concern for other people. Someone has likened a church to a gigantic sieve. Hundreds of hungry souls come looking for help but get so little attention that they slip right through our ranks without leaving a trace. If young people see their parents going out of their way to befriend newcomers at church, it is easy to get them to do the same in their youth groups, where love and acceptance are also often sadly lacking.

Space does not permit mention of all the other much-needed areas that provide us a place to serve the Lord in the church. Of one thing you can be certain: If you offer your talents to God, He will lead you to a meaningful ministry. Don't overlook the nursery, choir, or groups such as Pioneer Girls and Boys' Brigade. If you can't sing, be a choir mother for a children's or youth choir. Men can do repair and maintenance work on buildings and yard work on the grounds. Visitation and Sunday-school teaching are other options.

We hear a lot today about "involvement," and that is exactly what Christians should have in their churches. In such involvement they not only help others but are participating in the greatest work in the world.

Some time ago, a couple from our former church in Minneapolis dropped by for a visit. We talked of the day, twenty-five years before, when the Sunday-school superintendent and I had asked Bob, the husband, to teach a junior-department class of boys. We both laughed when I reminded him that after one year of teaching he candidly told me, "Pastor, I have learned more from teaching that class than I ever did listening to your sermons." Admitting that he was still teaching a class after all these years, he said, "Next to rearing my family, teaching is the most rewarding thing I do."

That man had the idea—and I couldn't help adding that teaching is one thing he does that will have eternal results.

The church provides many jobs like that for Spirit-filled Christians. What are you doing in *your* church?

10

Prayer Power for Family Living

The only problem in reading a book like this is that it exposes our weaknesses or failings and tends to leave us discouraged. Frequently we hear folks say after our Family Life Seminar, "I wish we had heard these principles years ago!" Our honest answer is—"So do we!" Fortunately we have some encouraging words for you . . . .

You Don't Have to Be Perfect!

No parent has ever been perfect. We certainly weren't! If Bev and I had our parenting days to live over, you can be sure we would do many things differently. I wish we had discovered the Spirit-filled life before our oldest child was fourteen—you can be sure we would have been better parents. But even then we wouldn't have been perfect. I wish we could say that since that thrilling experience at Forest Home, when God began to change our lives, we have been the ideal parents, but God and our children know better. There is no question that we are much improved. But per-

211

fect? I'm sorry to disillusion you. We weren't and still aren't.

Fortunately, God doesn't expect perfection, and neither do your children. The Bible teaches that "all have sinned and come short of the glory of God" (Romans 3:23). That includes even Christian parents. Because Spirit-filled Christians are not robots, we still give in to our old sin nature and react in the flesh on occasions. Hopefully, after studying this book you have gained the realization that—if you will quickly face and confess your sin—you will be immediately restored and *gradually* begin to "walk in the Spirit" on a regular basis. As you develop a keen sensitivity to sin, your times of carnality will become less frequent and "love, joy, peace, longsuffering, and goodness" will become a way of life.

The Christian Court of Last Appeals

A weeping wife and mother stopped me after a seminar and sobbed, "Is there any hope for a parent who has done everything wrong?"

"Of course!" I replied. Why? Because we Christians have resources that are unshared by any other group of people. What is that extra resource? *The power of prayer.*

You are doubtless familiar with the many challenges our Lord gave to prayer in the Gospels: "Ask, and it shall be given you; seek, and ye shall find . . . . For every one that asketh receiveth . . ." (Matthew 7:7, 8; ". . . whatsoever ye shall ask in prayer, believing, ye shall receive" (Matthew 21:22); ". . . ask, and ye shall receive, that your joy may be full" (John 16:24); ". . . men ought always to pray, and not to faint" (Luke 18:1); and many others. The Old Testament tells us: ". . . the prayer of the upright is his [God's] delight" (Proverbs 15:8).

In the Epistles of the New Testament we find scores of challenges to prayer: "Pray without ceasing" (1 Thessalonians 5:17); ". . . in every thing by prayer and supplication with thanksgiving let your requests be made known to God" (Philippians 4:6); ". . . The effectual fervent prayer of a righteous man availeth much" (James 5:16). As Christians we are privileged to address the supreme, omnipotent Creator of all things as "Dear Heavenly Father," for we have been adopted into the family of God. He has made us His children. Our Lord reassured us of God's interest in our prayers when He said, "If ye then, being evil, know how to give good gifts unto your children, how much more shall your Father which is in heaven give good things to them that ask him?" (Matthew 7:11).

All dedicated parents utilize this prayer power on behalf of their children at some time in their lives, particularly at times of great crises. Bev and I vividly recall standing at Lori's bedside when at the age of five she had her second bout with pneumonia. Her little chest was heaving as she gasped for every breath of life under the oxygen tent. Then the doctor said, "Preacher, if you've ever prayed in your life, you had better do it now—I've done all I can do. It is entirely up to God."

Bev wept as I prayed, and God gave us a supernatural "peace" that Lori would get well. In a matter of minutes she passed the crisis, and gradually the power of God restored her health. Almost all families face crises like this at some time during the growing-up years of their children. One of the many pluses of the Christian life is that we have someone real to turn to at such times. Frankly, I don't know how non-Christians make it.

Prayer is to a family what a roof is to a house; it protects those within from the enemies and adversities of life. In many cases, it even protects the family members from themselves—like the Christian wife who confided that while praying one morning she got the witness to her heart that her husband had been unfaithful. He had so carefully shielded himself from detection that she didn't have one clue of what he was doing, but she confidently faced him with his sin. He was so flabbergasted that he blurted out, "How did you know?" Her early detection and confrontation resulted in his repentance, and they have enjoyed years of happiness as a result.

Most of us in the ministry today are the result of someone else's prayers, and usually it is our parents'. In my own case it was my mother. Sensing that I had returned from the service extremely carnal and rebellious, she became prayerfully concerned. While attending a Bible conference she talked with Dr. Bob Jones, Sr., after his message one evening—and he prayed for her son Tim. A few weeks later I came home to her apartment at 2:30 A.M. and found my mother kneeling at the couch, sound asleep. The living room was so small I literally had to step across the back of her legs to get to my bedroom. At first it made me mad and I thought, "It serves her right; I'll leave her there!" But after getting into bed, I couldn't sleep. I knew she had to get up for work at 5:30 A.M., and that she no doubt was praying for me when she fell off to sleep. Finally I awakened her and she went to bed. That scene haunted me for days until I finally dropped my application to a prelaw school and went to Bob Jones University where my life was transformed. I wish every young man had that kind of a praying mother. Prayer won't make up for a lifetime of parental mistakes, but as a pastor I have witnessed life-changing miracles when burdened parents have sought God's power in the lives of their children.

Recently I encouraged another Christian worker, deeply concerned over two rebellious teenagers, that through

prayer these parents too had a court of last appeals. Sometimes our kids get so tired of hearing our sermons, that they
seem to become hardened to the things of the Lord. Into
each of our children's lives, He brought some other servant
of God at just the right time. Bev and I are deeply in debt to
such men as our good friend Ken Poure, well-known youth
and family-life speaker here in California; Pastor Jim Cook
of Hawaii; Bill Gothard; Pastor John McArthur; and, of
course, our own church's youth pastor, Jerry Riffe—plus
several others. These men, in response to our prayers, were
tools of the Holy Spirit to help our young people sort out
their thinking and recommit themselves to God at strategic
times in their lives. The Bible says, "Foolishness
[rebellion—which is as the sin of witchcraft] is bound in the
heart of a child; but the rod of correction will drive it far
from him" (Proverbs 22:15). In this rebellious age in which
we live, that spirit seems to be protracted. What is a parent
to do, even when he has made some mistakes? Prayer is the
answer! Spirit-controlled parents have power in prayer.

One of our children fell in love with another Christian (we
never permitted them to date non-Christians) who was not
really controlled by the Spirit. After praying about their
relationship, I became deeply burdened that it shouldn't
last, so I told Bev. Her eyes filled with tears and she said,
"The Lord has given me the same burden." After praying
together about it, we had a talk with our teen. I won't kid
you; the response was not pleasant! But we shared our
concern in love, and a few months later they lost interest in
each other. God has not given us these children to raise by
ourselves, but has left us the Bible—the best manual on
child raising and interpersonal relationships ever written—
and the power of prayer to help them on their way.

The most beautiful story along this line I have ever heard
was shared by a young architect in our church about his

youngest brother, Sam. It seems that he lost his Bible in the Northwest woods while on a camping trip with his parents. Another Christian family rented the cabin some time later and found the Bible but no name or address inside. They did find this inscription on the first page: "To our son with love, Mom and Dad." The couple was so impressed with this young man by reading the notes he had carefully written throughout his Bible that they called it to the attention of their children. That night at devotions the father prayed for this lad and then for his own teenage daughter—that someday the Lord would bring into her life a godly young man like the one who had owned the Bible.

Years passed and they all forgot the experience. Eventually their daughter grew up and fell in love with a fine young man she met in a college-age youth camp, and they became engaged. One month before their wedding the girl's parents were moving, and her fiancé came over to help them. As he picked up a box of books in the study, he saw an old Bible on the top. Setting the box down quickly, he examined it and exclaimed, "Where did you find my Bible?" Everyone was incredulous! Pointing to the inscription inside, he said, "See, it was given to me by my parents." Then, turning to the cover, he showed them the faded gold letters of his name, "Samuel"—but his last name had been worn off. It seems that these two Christian families, who lived over a hundred miles apart and did not know each other, had rented the same cabin that summer—one week apart.

Incredible? Impossible? With man, *yes*—with God, *anything is possible!*

Bev and I have no trouble believing that story, and neither does her mother, Mrs. Nell Ratcliffe. The Ratcliffe family joined the First Baptist Church of Farmington, Michigan, shortly after a young widow with three small children had moved to Detroit to live with relatives. Mrs.

Ratcliffe remembers the church women praying for "Margaret," the young widow. Because she had been widowed herself when Beverly was only eighteen months old, she was moved to pray for this unknown woman that God would supernaturally supply her many needs and enable her to raise her children to serve the Lord. Years passed; Bev and I met in college and were married. Several years later we were discussing backgrounds, and I happened to mention that our family had received Jesus Christ in the First Baptist Church of Farmington. We discovered that Bev's family had moved there two months after we left for Detroit. Would you believe my widowed mother's first name is *Margaret?*

Yes, God answers prayer. He loves you and wants you to use prayer as a tool of blessing for every member of your family.

Call upon me, and I will answer thee, and shew thee great and mighty things, which thou knowest not.

Jeremiah 33:3

Bibliography

Adams, Jay E. *Christian Living in the Home.* Grand Rapids, Michigan: Baker Book House, 1972.

Beardsley, Lou, and Spry, Toni. *The Fulfilled Woman.* Irvine, California: Harvest House, 1975.

Bowman, George M. *How to Succeed With Your Money.* Chicago, Illinois: Moody Press, 1960.

Burkett, Larry. *What Husbands Wish Their Wives Knew About Money.* Wheaton, Illinois: Victor Books, 1977.

Chandler, E. Russell. *Budgets, Bedrooms, and Boredom.* Glendale. California: Regal Books, 1976.

Chandler, Sandra S. *The Sensitive Woman.* Irvine, California: Harvest House, 1972.

Cooper, Darien B. *We Became Wives of Happy Husbands.* Wheaton. Illinois: Victor Books, 1976.

Daniels, Elam J. *How to Be Happily Married.* Orlando, Florida: Christ for the World Publishers, 1955.

Dobson, James. *Hide or Seek.* Old Tappan, New Jersey: Fleming H. Revell, 1974.

Drescher, John M. *Talking It Over.* Scottdale, Pennsylvania: Herald Press, 1975.

Fairfield, James G. T. *When You Don't Agree.* Scottdale, Pennsylvania: Herald Press, 1977.

Henry, Joseph B. *Fulfillment in Marriage.* Old Tappan, New Jersey: Fleming H. Revell, 1966.

Knecht, Mrs. Paul J. *For the Christian Home.* Chicago, Illinois: Moody Press, 1957.

LaHaye, Beverly. *How to Develop Your Child's Temperament.* Irvine, California: Harvest House, 1977.

_____. *The Spirit-Controlled Woman.* Irvine, California: Harvest House, 1976.

LaHaye, Tim. *How to Be Happy Though Married.* Wheaton, Illinois: Tyndale House, 1968.

————. *How to Win Over Depression.* Grand Rapids, Michigan: Zondervan, 1974.

————. *Spirit-Controlled Temperament.* Wheaton, Illinois: Tyndale House, 1966.

————. *Transformed Temperaments.* Wheaton, Illinois: Tyndale House, 1971.

————. *Understanding the Male Temperament.* Old Tappan, New Jersey: Fleming H. Revell, 1977.

————. *The Unhappy Gays: What Everyone Should Know About Homosexuals.* Wheaton, Illinois: Tyndale House, 1978.

LaHaye, Tim, and LaHaye, Beverly. *The Act of Marriage.* Grand Rapids, Michigan: Zondervan, 1976.

Larson, Bruce. *Marriage Is for Living.* Grand Rapids, Michigan: Zondervan, 1968.

MacDonald, Gordon. *Magnificent Marriage.* Wheaton, Illinois: Tyndale House, 1976.

McAllister, Jean et al. *Family Life.* Waco, Texas: Word Books, 1976.

McDonald, Cleveland. *Creating a Successful Christian Marriage.* Grand Rapids, Michigan: Baker Book House, 1975.

McMillen, S. I. *None of These Diseases.* Old Tappan, New Jersey: Fleming H. Revell, 1963.

Miller, Ella May. *I Am a Woman.* Chicago, Illinois: Moody Press, 1967.

Orr, William W. *How to Get Along With Your Parents.* Wheaton, Illinois: Scripture Press, 1958.

————. *What Every Christian Wife Should Know.* Wheaton, Illinois: Scripture Press, 1963.

Ortlund, Anne. *The Disciplines of a Beautiful Woman.* Waco, Texas: Word Books, 1977.

Ortlund, Ray, and Ortlund, Anne. *The Best Half of Life.* Glendale, California: Regal Books, 1976.

Price, Eugenia. *Woman to Woman.* Grand Rapids, Michigan: Zondervan, 1959.

Priddy, Eugene. *The Ideal Family.* Mount Freedom, New Jersey: Keynote Ministries, 1974.

Renich, Jill. *How to Find Harmony in Marriage.* Grand Rapids, Michigan: Zondervan, 1964.

Rice, John R. *The Home.* Grand Rapids, Michigan: Zondervan, 1946.

Rickerson, Wayne E. *Getting Your Family Together.* Glendale, California: Regal Books, 1976.

_____. *Good Times for Your Family.* Glendale, California: Regal Books, 1976.

Rinker, Rosalind. *How to Have Family Prayers.* Grand Rapids, Michigan: Zondervan, 1977.

Roberts, Doug. *To Adam With Love.* Van Nuys, California: Bible Voice, 1974.

Roberts, Roy R. *God Has a Better Idea—The Home.* Winona Lake, Indiana: BMH Books, 1975.

Small, Dwight Hervey. *After You've Said I Do.* Old Tappan, New Jersey: Fleming H. Revell, 1968.

Taylor, Florence M. *As for Me and My Family.* Waco, Texas; Word Books, 1976.

Taylor, Jack R. *One Home Under God.* Nashville, Tennessee: Broadman Press, 1974.

Timmons, Tim. *Maximum Marriage.* Old Tappan, New Jersey: Fleming H. Revell, 1976.

_____. *One Plus One.* Washington, D.C.: Canon Press, 1974.

Toffler, Alvin. *Future Shock.* New York, New York: Random House, 1970.

Wakefield, Norman. *You Can Have a Happier Family.* Glendale, California: Regal Books, 1977.

Wilke, Richard B. *Tell Me Again, I'm Listening.* Nashville, Tennessee: Abingdon Press, 1973.

Williams, Norman V. *The Christian Home.* Chicago, Illinois: Moody Press, 1952.

Wright, Norman. *An Answer to Family Communication.* Irvine, California: Harvest House, 1977.

_____. *Communication.* Glendale, California: Regal Books, 1974.

_____. *The Fulfilled Marriage.* Irvine, California: Harvest House, 1976.